LETTERS TO MITCH

LETTERS TO MITCH

THE HEALING POWER OF
GRIEF, LOVE & TRUTH

MARSHALL DUNN

For Mitch and my family...

Suffering is the most instructive teacher you have.
Your grief has its own power and intelligence.
Let it speak to you and tell you what it knows.

TABLE OF CONTENTS

INTRODUCTION:

WHEN YOUR MIND IS CLEAR, YOU HAVE NOTHING TO FEAR.

MY ELDER BROTHER Mitch completed suicide on October 1st, 2002. He was twenty-six years old. It was a month before my twenty-first birthday and my entire world flipped upside down. Things would never be the same. It was the end of a long chapter in my family's life with Mitch. We were left with fond memories in our hearts. We were also left with many years we'd all like to forget.

This is the story of what happened next, featuring a series of letters I wrote to my brother, Mitch, explaining how his suicide completely changed my outer world, steering me in a direction I never saw coming. Even more significantly, his death changed my inner world, opening me up to life's more meaningful and purposeful questions. Suffering led me to investigate the very essence of who I was, how I could heal, and how I could learn to embrace my true nature. As outrageous as it may sound, I can't thank Mitch enough for deciding to leave us.

There, I said it. Believe me, I never in my wildest dreams envisioned myself saying those words. But that was before I understood the nature of existence and how to live my truth in the midst of a trail of destruction. That was before I really got to know Mitch, after he checked out from this physical plane. Despite the twenty years I spent under the same roof with him, only now can I see the truth about Mitch. With my new pair of eyes comes intense clarity, as I see life and death with an open heart, willing to honor my own gift of life. Mitch was my spark. The life-altering insights I gained are because of him and I thank him every day.

The day that Mitch died, I was hopeless, brimming with fear, and utterly numb. Confronted with death, I was scared, I was alone, I was angry, I was guilty, I was ashamed, I was deeply saddened, I was lost, I was weak, and I was confused. Most of all, I had no idea who I was. I might as well have been dead myself. In essence, I was a living, breathing corpse, muddling my way through a world in which I viewed the permanence of life as a preordained plan. I was wrapped up in the pursuit of the trivial because I didn't know any better. Combine that with excessive drinking and partying. While I was figuring out what the hell to do with my life, I turned into a zombie on the inside, remaining well-masked to everyone on the outside.

It felt like I died with Mitch but in truth, a part of me was born to a new life, a part that had lain dormant like a sleeping volcano. I was invited to open a door inside of me that had the potential to transform my life – a life that I came to know as the Truth of who I am. Initially, though, it felt like a void. I thought that void was Mitch after he had checked out as my brother.

I was incorrect. The void was the absence of my truth, a window into my purpose, the first step on a new path that I didn't really choose and it was far from clear. I only knew that I needed to trust and explore deeper. Without trust, I would not be sitting here today at the base of the Hollywood Hills in Los Angeles in an empty living room with no furniture except a small wooden chair and a table on which to assemble this book.

Today, I can see that Mitch gave me the opportunity of a lifetime – the opportunity to know myself, something I might not have done if he hadn't passed. These days, it gives me great pleasure to write, coach, speak, and connect with people from all over the world as I help them peel back the layers of their own suffering. I encourage them to remember the Divine love within and to do what is necessary to unlock their purpose-driven lives.

Through Mitch's suicide, a door to inspired creativity and a curiosity about the universe was thrown open. It had its intense struggles and inner battles. I had to get real in order to heal. I had to find the willingness to dive into the agony that exposed my insecurities, including ugliness and pain from the past. I was caught between two worlds – wanting to heal my life and taking action. For many of us, the old ways are too difficult and familiar to leave behind. In my case, I felt a dull comfort in suffering, even when I knew deep down that it wasn't serving me. I knew I wasn't honoring the life and the unconditional love that was my gift at birth. On paper, these were the most terrifying years of my life. In reality, they turned out to be the most liberating.

Mitch's death led me to explore many countries and cultures. It also led me to explore my inner world in silence – a world where I have everything I need, where I am complete, where everything is in balance and in divine order. Mitch's passing has introduced me to wonderful people who have become great friends, colleagues, mentors, and lovers. I cannot begin to comprehend the extent of the web of interrelatedness and synchronicity since his death, but I love it and I am forever grateful to him. Our family unit has become stronger in many ways. We aren't saints and we have each dealt with our grief in different ways, but our core has remained sturdy. Relationships with close friends have more depth now because Mitch opened the doors to sensitivity and compassion in a way I never imagined was possible. He encouraged me to open my heart and to express myself without judgment. His death has inspired authenticity in my life and it has brought me new love.

Above all, Mitch taught me that death is a continuation of life. Due to the onset of eerie appearances to family members, vivid and penetrating dreams, a deeper connection to nature, heightened self-awareness and a stronger spiritual relationship with Mitch than ever before, I understand that he has taken on a different form. His physical container may have been buried, but his soul lives on, one of the main reasons I'm writing this book.

There have been times when in a sense, I was trying to take my own life with alcohol, drugs, bad relationships, soul sucking jobs, careless behavior, a lack of presence, and slavery to my negative mind. These are all wicked games. At times, I exhibited the very qualities in Mitch that I hated – laziness, keeping secrets, self-abuse, and the self-destructive, self-pitying waste of my natural talent. I have felt a turbulent bubble of emotion that was ready to burst and flood my garden of life with poisonous weeds.

Now, I can clearly see how those times, qualities, and emotions served and benefited me. My perceptions and beliefs have shifted and that has made all the difference. Mitch's death has made me more aware of my thoughts and what I feed my mind. He has helped me create balance in my life. Yes, his suicide has helped me create balance. I have learned how to find equilibrium in the new world he gave me. I have put to bed the same old stories that constantly ran around in my head, creating nothing but negativity, pain, and suffering. I have seen and done all of this because of Mitch's death.

I no longer view grief as bad or something that defines my life. To me, grief is guidance, it is a skill, a wake up call to return to love. I have come to feel grateful for the choice my brother made and I can see the gifts he gave me – the gift of re-birth, the gift of wholeness, the gift of clarity, the gift of purpose, the gift of empathy, the gift of compassion, and the gift of knowing myself and what I have to offer this world. Finally, he gave me the ultimate gift – my life as it was meant to be lived. And now, I can offer hope and inspiration to people on their own healing paths in the midst of personal challenges.

Mitch doesn't need my forgiveness, nor do I need his. There is nothing to forgive. He took his life and opened up mine and the lives of those around me. His death awakened love in all of us and I don't hate him. I'm not angry or frustrated any longer. I'm not guilty or sad because his death has offered me something as beautiful as the birth of a child. Of course, there is a natural time to mourn the loss of any relationship, but when I stay focused on the truth, I see that love remains by my side.

The pages of this book detail the fraught journey I embarked upon when my brother died, and how I eventually got to a better place. Maybe you will be able identify with some of it or all of it. Maybe it will spark a new conversation among yourself and others. Maybe it will help you shift your perspective, and it might even save your life. I've learned that there is a hidden order to everything and we have to embrace change and expand with the universe. We are not separate from each other or from anyone or anything else. If you are reading this book, I sincerely hope I can help open your eyes to the Truth so you can live a richer, fuller and more inspired life like I'm doing now. "Now" is all we have ever had and all we ever will have. Let's be present for it.

Live from love,

Marshall

In the night you pass by
With a message to let go
A heart of breath
An open palm
A star within shines its truth
In the night you pass by
With a message there's no goodbye…

– M.D.

PART ONE:
HERE COMES FEAR

LETTER 1:
BROKEN IN HALF

October, 2002

Dear Mitch,

A SUNKEN EMPTINESS possesses my soul. We were a family of six, now we're five, but we might as well be none because you're gone. I wish this hellish experience was a deception, an illusion behind the veil of reality where I thought we so happily lived.

Knock, knock.

Who's there?

Police.

Police who?

Police come back with good news that you're alive and well.

Yes, the boys in blue did knock at 0'dark hundred. I heard the door. I was too comfortable to lift myself from underneath the covers. Someone else will get the door, I thought, as my eyes closed and I dozed – until I felt the pressure of a body sitting by my side. Mum. I felt her gentle touch. I opened one eye in the darkness and there she was in her robe, her face sunken. It was Mum, your Mum, my Mum, our Mum. Mum. She didn't have to say anything. It was written all over her face.

"He was such a troubled soul. Such a troubled, troubled soul," I heard her say.

I was crushed by her words. I have no clue how it feels to outlive your own child. Or to take your life, this gift given to you, which will never be fully expressed. I can hear all of this in Mum's broken heart that beats to a different rhythm on this night and will continue to do so for many nights to come. She has always been here for all of us. She and I hold each other. I feel the unconditional love a mother has for her children and a paralyzing crush of fear gives rise. That's when I feel your blindsided King Hit. Thank you for this shattering introduction to death, Mitch, you selfish bastard.

I can't leave my room. I can't turn onto my side. I'm frozen. I'm stuck to the bed in a waking nightmare. The mattress feels like a magnet against my back, strapping me down. I'm breathing but I don't know I am. I'm scared. I'm switched off. Am I really here right now? Is this actually happening? Would someone please walk back into my room and tell me this is a sick joke? Mitch, call my phone. You'll do that for me, right?

Mitch?

I knew you could hit hard on the rugby field, smashing the opposition any time you had the opportunity. But your family? We're short a player now. How are we supposed to win at this game of life? Your King Hit smacked me across the back of my head and cracked every bone in my body, knocking me out into a dribbling vegetable. I'd ask for help from the family, but they're sitting next to me in the same lounge room, staring out the same window. We're suddenly in our nineties. We're like a family of dementia patients sitting in our wheelchairs with old knitted blankets on our laps, gazing at spots on the wall that seem to hold some significance. Where are the full-time caretakers? Everything's busted, Mitch, but I can't feel the pain. Not yet, big brother. I'm so far beyond pain right now. You've teleported me to hell. The closets are open. Can you see all the skeletons falling out onto the floor? Every time I glance over at Mum and Dad or Matt and Morg, I can see that it's a shambles between their ears. A tidal wave of fear bigger than Jack's beanstalk has landed on the roof of this house, cracking the foundations. So this is what it feels like when a family member decides he doesn't want to live anymore. What kind of messed up, dark and lonely space would you have to be in to do this to yourself and to us? We were brothers, man.

You'd been missing for the last two days. It was some story about you being out of town. When did you ever go out of town? Where is out of town? And still, the alarm bells weren't ringing in my head. The story didn't sound too far-fetched, but then again, seventeen thousand dollars missing from a business account to which you had access, pricked our ears. No, no, surely Mitch wouldn't have done something like that. I'm sure you wouldn't have done that to Dad, the great man who stood by you and loved you from the day he first cradled you in his arms. You did, though. It was your last hurrah before you were shot down in a blaze of glory.

I did forget about you, Mitch. Is that how you felt for these last ten years, forgotten about? I didn't connect the dots. Oh, God. What have we done?

The house is full of people, so you know they care about you, too. Is this the attention you longed for? Everyone's here – family, close friends, old friends, neighbors. They're all here with flowers and food. There isn't anything these poor people can say. Take a look at them. My best mate, Paul, is here. I mean, what the hell can he say? I'm being showered with hugs and warmth but I'm shivering cold. I'm an ice sculpture. That, or I'm a newborn again – helpless. I'm walking, but I can't feel my legs moving or my bare feet on the hardwood floors in the dining room, or out on the lush green grass that Mum keeps perfectly manicured. People are talking to me but I'm deaf. It honestly sounds like we're all underwater.

My mouth is a desert. I'm looking at all these close friends and family, but I'm not actually seeing anyone. It's as if these rooms full of people are waves of energy moving around. I can't make out anything. I know I look pale, even though I've been in the sun all week, swimming at Balmoral Beach, having the time of my life. You know my life, Mitch – easy, breezy, Japanezy. Three bar shifts a week, a handful of hours at university, a beautiful girlfriend, and no rent to pay. I have no idea what I want to do with my life, but who cares? I like smooth sailing. I like the calm waters. I love my life. I *did* fucking love my life.

I can't look anyone in the eye now, including my girlfriend, Elle, and least of all, myself. There's no chance in hell I'm looking in the mirror any time soon. Oh my Lord, not the mirror. I'm not stepping foot inside a bathroom. It's become a torture chamber. I'll go outside and water Mum's plants if nature calls. Who knows what this guy looks like at the moment?

I'm a distant version of the guy swimming at the beach with his mates a few days ago, eyeing girls in bikinis, sipping mixed berry smoothies.

You're a real prick, you know that? I've never seen Dad cry. Ever. You know how he gets with anything remotely emotional. It's a trip into a new dimension for him. He's free-falling into a black hole. My heart breaks into more pieces when I look at the big man doing his best. I can't imagine what Mum and Dad are feeling right now. Suicide has crashed into our twin towers of strength. The explosion. The smoke. Do we jump out the windows with you? This family unit has become Ground Zero. Did you even stop for a second to think what this would do to us? The guilt, the shame, the regrets. I mean, Mitch, those two gave you everything. They tried everything to help you. But no, you self-pitying son of a bitch. You couldn't help yourself. Did you even try? Was it too hard for you? It must have been, because you bowed out a defeated young man. That's not the Mitch I used to know. Then again, that seems like another lifetime. The brother I knew died a long time ago.

You know what just hit me? Oh, you'll love this. This is the *crème freche* with Mum's brownie straight out of the oven at Sunday lunch, big brother. Everyone's going to be looking at me to do the eulogy at the funeral. Beautiful. Who else is going to do it? Mum or Dad? Forget that. They're a shivering mess. Morgan? He just lost his big brother and best friend. The poor bloke is more broken than any of us. I don't think he's opened his mouth since he heard the news. Matthew? If I can find his head that spun off his neck at a billion revolutions per second, that may be an option, but it's highly unlikely.

Me? Well of course it's fucking me. What do I say? I can't even remember what you were like growing up – the happy times before those dark clouds circled above you and pissed down a rain so depressing, it flooded you and the rest of the family. Right, so I'm doing the eulogy. I'll say all the wonderful things I'm supposed to say. He was this, he was that, gone too soon, blah-blah-blah. What I really want to say is – Oh, Christ. Just forget it. These feelings will pass some day and we'll crack open the champagne and celebrate the life you lived. Yeah, that day might come but you can bet your bottom dollar it's not gonna be anytime soon. In the meantime, we're rolling out the black carpet because the Premiere of Death is now showing. Can't wait to see how this one ends.

We're down at the beach now, having some calamari and chips. Usually they're my favorites. Today they don't taste the same. The fresh air and the grace of the ocean distracts me from the numbness a little bit. Your death has been a lot to take in and far from digestible. Matt, Morg, and I sit on a bench with our tasteless food. We are at a loss. Three on a bench feels off balance. Is that how it'll be for the rest of this lifetime without you? Do we search for answers? Where do we go from here? I look over at Matt and Morg and then out to sea. I wonder how this will change us. Who am I really? Life moves forward and it always will. You passed away during this speck of time and things will continue on. Only now life is different. I have to wonder – what does it all mean?

Let me ask you again, big brother. What the hell happens to us now?

Marsh

MITCH LEAVES EVERYTHING DIFFERENT

YOU NEVER DREAM of something like this happening. Then it hits you and everything is different. Everyone on this Earth dies at some point. At twenty years old, however, I never really contemplated it. Why would I, when living was so much fun?

We were living in Balmoral at the time of Mitch's passing. It was a gentle stroll of a few hundred meters to the beach, a really gorgeous part of the world in Sydney Harbor. The house was flooded with endless natural sunlight, which lit up my face every time I walked through the front door. Mum put so much love and care into making it feel like a family home, you never wanted to leave. It was delicious and cozy. Only Morg and I still lived at home. Matt and Mitch weren't too far away in their own one-bedroom apartments. Mitch had expressed interest that he wanted to move back home. Mum and Dad said no. Mitch wasn't happy about that — he felt rejected. I don't think it helped his self-loathing attitude that had already crippled his way of being in the world. I understood Mum and Dad's stance. Living with his heaviness over the past eight years had sucked the life out of them.

That's why I was so angry initially. I was numb, I was in shock, I was scared, I was all those things and more — and I was very, very angry. Why did Mitch have to cast the darkest of shadows on this house and take away the endless natural light? Fuck him. I thought he wanted to sabotage our lives. He was so unhappy in his own, and if he was going to suffer, then so were we. That was my logic at the time. Suicide loss can really mess with your head like that. You want to point the finger and blame it on someone or something. You want answers. You want clarity. You want information. And when you get none of that, it literally drives you mad. You're left with nothing, except the reality of moving on with life. The question is – how can anyone move on after such a devastating loss? Other questions, both haunting and terrifying, are:

Will I ever be okay?

How will this change me? Change us?

Will I ever get over it?

How long will I be in this state of grief?

Will his loss affect my growth in life?

What does life look like now?

How do I make meaning from this?

All these questions revolved around my family and me because we were the ones left standing in the overwhelming sadness of losing a brother and a son. The poor guy had lost his light. He was defeated and desperate and saw only one way out. The physical container with which he'd been blessed must have felt like a prison. And then, I found myself in my own prison of guilt, shame, blame, anger, and isolation. How long was my sentence?

That week, I was meant to sit my end of year university finals exams. I was in the first year of a Bachelor of Arts program at Macquarie University in which I had little interest to begin with. I was "getting my piece of paper," so to speak. My mind was empty and dull and still, it was racing with questions. It was a weird feeling that I can only describe as "shock." I was so out of it, I could have sat a third grade math exam and I probably would have failed. Twenty times five equals what? Numb had made me dumb. I picked up the phone to call my professors and haltingly told them what had happened. They assured me that everything would be okay and I didn't have to sit the exams. Gratefully, they passed me anyway.

It felt like I was broken in half. Half of me wanted to run and hide and pretend none of it ever happened. The other half wanted Mitch back so badly. I was sure we could help fix whatever the problem was and once again, we could all be happy together. I just didn't understand that the only person who can heal you is you.

LETTER 2:

WIPE THAT SMILE OFF YOUR FACE

October, 2002

Dear Mitch,

I'VE INSANELY DECIDED to go to the morgue with Matt to view your soulless corpse. I know I'm impulsive. Decision-making is not my strong suit, especially after smoking pot most days for the past month. Mum and Dad drove together in one car and Matt and I were in the other. Morg stayed at home. Smart move. He's always been cautious like that. I can see him in the kitchen now, having a glass of milk with two butterscotch finger biscuits. It's simple. It works for him.

In the car, we switch on the radio to break up the silence. What's playing? The *Eurogliders* are singing, *"Heaven Must Be There."* Is it now?

I'm not sure what I'm hoping to achieve from this visit besides eternal nightmares. Everything is so still, so quiet, so dead in the morgue. It feels haunted. The stench of death emanates from the carpet floor. I'm with Dad and the funeral director and it feels like a scene out of the HBO series, *Six Feet Under.* We sit in a cold office and pick a casket from a catalogue. The bile in my stomach climbs into my throat (it feels worse than a tequila hangover) when I decide to join Mum and Matt in the viewing room. That term, "the viewing room," sounds like we're about to take in something beautiful. But today, it isn't the Grand Canyon. The only canyon is the void inside of me. Dad stays put in the office. I don't think he can handle seeing your body. Or maybe he saw it before I arrived. I'm not sure. Details are sketchy at best.

There you are, lying flat on a dolly bed, fast asleep forever. Good night sweet prince. You loved a good sleep-in, didn't you? Or those long, hot thirty to forty minute showers where you'd sit on the slate tiles underneath the warm water, singing Pink Floyd. You must be in paradise, you shit.

A terrifying reality sets in that I'm staring at you, my dead brother. Congratulations on being the first and only dead person I've ever seen. I stand arm in arm with Mum, her body trembling as she sobs. I slowly reach down to touch your head. Shit, it's cold. I quickly pull my hand back as if I'm being shocked with electricity. There's something weird about all this. Yeah, okay, you're dead in front of me but why do you look so happy? I turn to Mum and Matt. Are they seeing this? For a brief moment I feel a sense of comfort but it quickly turns into mental and emotional rage. You're smiling?! What's so funny? You look so peaceful, so relieved. You have a high-and-mighty grin on that smug face of yours, the same expression you made when you farted while we were watching TV. You're dead and you're bloody smiling at us, rubbing it in our faces. "Doesn't he look happy?" Mum remarks.

"He does," I say.

What the hell is that about? I need to drill deeper here. What exactly are you smiling about? Does this give you some kind of satisfaction? Well, I'm glad it all worked out okay for you. You realize you've torn Mum's heart in half, don't you? What's so funny? I'm baffled. My eyes are locked on you, Pal, and I want to know what is so bloody funny. Did your stealthy calculating mind have this all planned out? The final shindig, the party for one, full of alcohol, hookers and drugs. *Bon voyage*, world, it's been real. No note to us, no nothing. I'm glad you gave yourself the five star treatment and a little pampering before the last call. Goin' out in style, brother! This is unbelievable.

I take a few deep breaths and calm down. I know I'm looking at this from my personal perspective and not taking into account for a second what you were going through. You were doing so well, but if you'd slipped into desperation, why didn't you come to us? We knew it was hard for you. What couldn't you say to your own family? There had to have been something more we could have done. You asked me to go see a movie with you a few weeks back, which we hadn't done since I was sixteen. I told you I had plans with Elle. If I'd known that was the last time we'd ever spend time together, I would have had a choc-top with you in the cinema while we watched the latest Spielberg film. I thought at the time it was a bit strange that you were asking me to hang out. "Why?" was the only word that came to mind. I know the answer now. That was it, huh? That was going to be our last brother hang wasn't it? I missed it. We all missed it.

Now you're smiling at us. Are you finally free – free of whatever you were holding onto that poisoned the garden? I can see the light in you now. There's no more darkness. Does this mean the light was always there, buried in some corner of your being? If it was buried, why didn't you dig it back up? Look at you, you're happy! Is that what your face is telling me? No? I'm sure the owners of the morgue didn't paint that smile on you. It's like a layer was peeled back, the curtain dropped, and ta-da! Here *you* are. No resistance. I see peace. I see Mitch. The Mitch we used to know. What does that mean? What created that awful layer? What created that false identity and why did you buy into that feeling, that existence? You were born with a brilliant mind and a sensitivity that was in tune with your fellow brothers. Why couldn't you remember your magnificence?

The ride home with Matt has me thinking about that smile of yours. It's the one BIG thing I miss about you. You had a smile that could light up a room, cliché as it sounds. That smile would have come in handy to light up that dark room inside your mind during those last stormy years. In all the photos of us as kids, you were always the one with the biggest smile. You were the best looking of the bunch. You shined so brightly as a kid and into your early teens. Were you too bright for this world? Was that smile that opened up the gates to heaven telling us something? Did you know all along?

When I think about it now, you always had an unfathomable sensitivity about everything in this world. Now you're smiling like you know everything about life, peering down on us like you know the truths of the universe. You know the other side. You know God. You know everything. Is that why you're smiling? Should we be smiling with you, is that it? What are you trying to tell us? It feels like a puzzle right now, a Rubik's Cube we're going to have to figure out as individuals and as a family. Where the hell is that going to lead us? In what direction? The right direction? Who are we, really? And death – what do we do about that? It's coming for everyone. Do we talk about it? I'm searching, Mitch. I'm really searching.

All I know right now is that you've opened up a can of worms inside me. It's nauseatingly unfamiliar and twitchingly uncomfortable. I can't see much through my current fog, but a pilot has been lit for something. It's the oddest feeling. I feel a surge of energy rising up from my innermost core. By the time it reaches my throat, I push it back down. I have no clue what that is. I don't think I've had much of a clue about anything since I left school. One thing's for sure, though – life is fragile and some of us leave sooner than others. It had to be you, didn't it?

Tell me more about that smile.

Marsh

REFLECTION:

MITCH TEACHES ME TO INQUIRE

YOU SEE YOUR brother at peace with a smile on his face at the morgue after he's taken his own life, and yes, you have the right to say, "Today is a very strange day." It's a different day from all other days. In the world of movies, this would be the inciting incident. I am the hero in this movie, which is my life, and my journey literally starts now. The ease on Mitch's face sparks inquiry, posing questions I've never pondered in my life. These questions are propelling my curiosity and thirst for knowledge and insight. At a time when my energy levels are depleted, there is a tiny flame of inspiration.

God comes to mind. What does God mean to me? Do I believe in Him? What is my relationship to Him? What does it feel like to be connected to Him? Do I have blocks around a connection to God? Is Mitch happy because he's free? Has he merged back with God and is he cavorting with the other souls?

Every day we're faced with a million choices. Some seem relatively insignificant, like which TV program I should watch this evening. Other have life-changing significance. In this case, the question was, should I ride with Matt to the morgue and view Mitch's body, or should I stay home and never have that image in my mind? If I'd decided not to go the morgue, would I still have directed my consciousness towards spiritual-inquiry? I hazard a guess I probably would have, but the choice to see Mitch and what I gained from that experience, although shocking and nightmarish, helped me take the next step. I couldn't see the whole staircase to my journey after his death, but seeing his body gave me the courage to inquire and that became my next step.

For someone else, that experience might have been interpreted differently. But I believe major life events offer us a universal invitation for inner-inquiry. Intuitively, that's what I was told in the moment. By whom? By someone, something that lives inside me that sees. I can only describe it as spirit. Whether or not to accept the invitation is a choice. I may think deeper than some, I may see things others don't, and I may feel an intimate connection to my spirit, but life is life. We're all in it. We're all the same. I believe that at some level we're all connected. We have to be. I'm just a guy who lost his brother to suicide and I'm trying to figure out what to do next. In time that will come.

Going to see Mitch was a good thing.

LETTER 3:

DEATH AT A FUNERAL

October, 2002

Dear Mitch,

It's closing in on forty degrees Celsius outside. Of course we have to dress in black for your departure. Not only are we covered in guilt, shame and regret. We also have on a generous slap of SPF sunscreen.

I slept for thirty-two seconds last night. Every time I closed my eyes, I kept seeing Mum sitting at the edge of my bed in her robe that kept her shivering body from turning to ice. Her whimpering words, "He was such a troubled soul," echoed in my head. Words that I fear will echo in my head for many nights to come. Rested or not, I know this day will forever be stamped in my mind. I just never imagined it would come this soon.

You should see all the people who are here to wave goodbye to you. People cared about you, you know? Through my dark shades I wonder who all these wonderful people are. It's funny how we all come together as a community, old faces from the schoolyard, the various childhood neighborhoods, parents, teammates, ex-girlfriends, and the list goes on. We come together, we share our grief, we say our goodbyes, and we're all horrified about our own numbers being called. Is this our way of preparing for death?

I doubt you saw a single friend outside of us on your last birthday. The two common denominators in this congregation are "old" and "ex." I don't think you knew many people after your teenage years – no one who actually cared about you. Then again, why would someone take the time to get to know you and care about you when you couldn't have given a rat's arse about yourself? That self-pitying "the-world-is-against-me" attitude. How could this world and our loving family that begged you to see your own magnificence be against you? God, what happened to that beautiful mind of yours? Do you have any clue how incredibly talented you were?

You'll be happy to know that your casket lies perfectly at the base of the altar. You're large, in charge, and holding court. For such a big stage without an empty seat in the church, the silence is deafening. The dominant energy among us is the trembling beat of everyone's frightened heart. You are putting us all into some kind of terror cell as you force us to question the so-called "normalcy" of life. You are challenging our upstanding attitudes to life and we are defenseless, Mitch.

Oh Christ, I'm having another moment. How the hell did this just happen? We're sitting in the front row huddled together, our arms interlocked. Our family is missing a vital piece and you're in a big wooden rectangular box in front of us, fast asleep. Can you please wake up, Mitch? I'm too spun out right now to even think about the fact that I'm doing the eulogy. My legs are shaking. I'm paranoid I'll swallow my tongue. Another thirty-two seconds of sleep last night would have come in handy, now that I think about it. You know those nightmares where you want to scream for help but nothing comes out and no one comes to help? I'm pretty sure I'm in one of them now, only in this nightmare, if you want to vomit up and down the church aisles, you can.

But look! Look at all the beautiful, colorful flowers neatly arranged on the casket. They're nice. I like them. As I said, all the Dunns are in the front row – a first in our church. The three times you ever sit in the first row in a church are a mass where you're saying a Prayer of the Faithful, a family wedding, and a family death. Those are the three times I can recall. Mum's been inconsolable for the past few days, which seem to have passed in slow motion. It *may* have been three days. I'm just guessing, I have no clue, to be honest. We're blessed to have so many great friends here to support us. I don't know how we would cope without them. They've kept us fed when we can't stomach so much as half a piece of toast.

Mum asked for a priest from St. Aloysius to conduct the service. He keeps slipping on your name, making a real Wally of himself, calling you Marsh or Matt or Martin. Usually, this would be embarrassing, but today no one seems to care. Everyone is too busy wiping eyes and blowing noses. It's way too many "M" names to remember for anyone, especially on stage in a packed, eerily quiet church during a service about a life that is gone too soon. You're someone who fell into the shadows and never stepped back into the light. Did you forget that the sun rises every morning?

My eyes zoom in on your casket. The life that you lived flashes before my eyes. I see you driving the Boston Whaler across the still waters of the harbor, your blonde wavy hair blowing in the breeze. Bit of a male model you were. You're wearing braces, but who hasn't in this family? We can thank Mum and Dad for those crappy dental genes. I see you watching me playing under 8's rugby, the game you truly loved, yelling encouragement from the sidelines. I see you in the pool doing somersaults off the diving board. I see you and Morg together, the best of friends. I see you eating your beloved peanut butter on toast and loving every bite. I see you singing to *Credence Clearwater Revival* in your room. You sound nothing like Mr. Fogerty, but you're in love with every beat. I see you with pretty girls in high school. I see you again and again and again and the sun is always shining in a clear blue sky. If the sun is always shining, how can there be room for these dark clouds?

When the priest calls me for the eulogy, I almost run out the door. Some kind of inner strength magically carries my wobbly legs to the lectern. This is actually happening, I think to myself. One second, you're poking me in my side which you know I hate, as I hungrily grab a handful of shaved turkey from the fridge. The next, you're all packed up in that box in front of my eyes, dead. I saw you last week, for Christ sake.

I walk past your casket on my way to the lectern to speak my parting words. I can hear you singing in my head. Okay, you sound a smidge like John Fogerty. I'll give you that. I've written down a speech on a piece of paper and it's folded in my jacket pocket. I take it out but I forget how to read. Words? Paper? Words on paper? People in front of me? I have to talk? Talking? I guess this is how a doped up patient's brain in the psych ward operates. Have I written down everything I want to say? No. I hesitate a minute. I wait for that moment of inspiration where I imagine scrunching up the piece of paper, tossing it to the side, and delivering a jaw dropping reality check that could be Oscar nominated for Best Male Eulogy in a Family Suicide Film.

In my imagined speech, I speak with complete clarity and insight into living the best life. I talk about the eternal truth of death and how suicide can be prevented through a deeper connection to ourselves and family, not the modern day world of technology and materialism. I tell everyone how that desperate, unattainable, hollow need for more can be replaced with more listening and compassion for each other. I tell my audience how we can hear what's going down inside and we can talk through any problem or challenge.

But that moment doesn't come. Instead, I talk about you. Who Mitch was to me. You were my big brother. The one who taught me how to tackle on the rugby field. The big brother that I looked up to as a kid. The big brother that watched over Morgan and me, the babies of the family. The big brother who had such deep sensitivity and empathy for others. The big brother with whom I shared a mutually respectful relationship. The big brother that will now be the first thing I think about in the morning and the last thing at night. I deliver the best talk I can in front of a room of long faces wrapped up in their own fears about this life. When will it be my turn? Is that what everyone is thinking?

I'll never forget carrying your casket down the aisle and out to the black hearse waiting patiently on the street. Your departing song from the church, *I'll Stand By You* by *The Pretenders*, will forever bring me to a reflective standstill. The day we are saying goodbye to you. The day our lives take a different form. As I start the journey down the aisle, I'm looking at my mate, Paul, whose face is crying tears for both himself and me because mine aren't ready to break through the barricade of shock. In Paul's face I see true friendship, something I wish I had with you Mitch, instead of brotherly mutual respect. We were always so close to taking our relationship further. Why didn't we cross that bridge? Do you think we can work on our relationship now that you're gone? Will you speak to me?

There's that blue sky again as your casket is carefully loaded into the hearse. That beautiful, blue Sydney sky strikes an unforgettable chord within me. Next week, it may be rainy or cloudy, but it's still the same sky. It will change each and every day but it will always remain the sky.

You left us, Mitch, and you won't be the last to do so. Friends will go and eventually more family will go. They will go and go and go and go. Then new life will come. It will come and come and come and come. It will come and it will go, but it will always be life. Just as the sky changes, so does life. Nothing is ever fixed.

At the cemetery, the sun is peaking through with its stinging hot rays. A small, tightknit gathering of close friends and family watch you being lowered into your new bedroom. It's dark – the way you like it. One massive sleep-in coming right up! I wonder if God will tap you on the shoulder and send you back here for another stint? I wonder. Or will you be a gentlemen and wait for the rest of us? I'm pretty sure you have some explaining to do. Did you ever think about reincarnation before you commended yourself to eternal sleep? Personally, I'd like to come back as a dolphin, but that's just me. You may have prayed for something better, but don't be fooled. What you had with us was special.

Before we close your bedroom door with soil, the priest asks each of us to take a flower from the wooden basket at his feet. We are supposed to say a final prayer to you and drop the flower on the hood of your casket. It feels like a wishing well as I watch everyone kiss their flower and release it from their shaky hands. I wonder if everyone has the same wish for you? I hope you feel the power of love breaking through this outpouring of grief. Feel it, use it, and come back to the light.

I stand behind Mum, while she witnesses what any parent would dread. I'm at a loss to even imagine where she is in her head. I know her heart is broken. Our Mum's heart is broken. I never believed that fortress could crumble. My hand rests upon her shoulders that are burdened with guilt, like the rest of us, and I wondered if we'll all be okay. What does okay mean, anyway? Were we okay before you died? Were we ever okay? As we lay you down to rest for this long, eternal night, aren't we also laying to rest this family as it used to be? Is your death the death of us, of this unit? We shower each day to wash the dirt off so we can start afresh. Is your death the cold shower we need to wash away any ominous clouds of doubt, regret, shame, and guilt holding us back from love and growth?

You've exposed us, Mitch. Now we don't know anything. There is no certainty. You've left us naked and vulnerable. If we are to die here with you as a family and give life to something else, something greater, something more loving and more powerful, who will we see in the mirror when we look at ourselves? Who and what are we going to see? You've stripped us down to our bare bones and all I can feel is fear. I feel disconnected from myself. I love you as a brother, so why do I feel that love has left me? Where is this fear coming from? In another corner of my psyche, I can feel the warmth of hope. I feel it in Mum's quivering touch as she reaches back over her shoulder and touches my hand. Love returns with that touch for a split second. My heart smiles as best it can. Rest in peace.

You've sucked me into a new world, Mitch. I'm scared shitless of who I'll see inside. I hate you for leaving. I hate you for what's to come: the unknowns of life without you, of living with suicide, of discovering my deep yearning for truth. I love my comforts. I love it safe. I love it warm and fuzzy. I love this... illusion? I better come out the other side in one piece.

Life is so fragile. Your passing is so abrupt. One day you're in the kitchen with me, the next I'm carrying you on my shoulders out of a church. What just happened? I'm peering into the rabbit hole, Mitch. How deep does this thing go?

Is this our final goodbye?

Marsh

MITCH TEACHES ME TO EMBRACE CHANGE

WE'RE SURROUNDED BY change. Yesterday was different from today and tomorrow will be different, too. The weather changes on a daily basis. Leaves grow on trees and then fall away. Flowers bloom and then they wither. Our physical bodies change with age. You're not looking at the same physical body in the mirror that you saw five years ago.

Our relationships change, as well. Some people stay together for the long haul and grow together. Some relationships dissolve after a brief moment in time. Careers change. Your taste buds change when suddenly, you fancy red wine. What you value also changes, depending on your current stage of life. When you become a partner and/or a parent, your priorities shift from the single life to the family unit. What I'm saying here is that our world changes and expands endlessly. We all live and then we die, just like everything else around us.

The death of Mitch was the biggest change I ever faced. Why do we have trouble embracing death if it's a natural process of life? The more I contemplated this question over time as I worked to heal my heart and mind, the more I wanted to live in the moment. In a world of constant flux, I knew I couldn't predict what would happen today or tomorrow. That didn't mean that every time I walked outside, I was anxious about being blindsided by a bus or being attacked by a crazy person. In fact, it had the opposite effect. Contemplating death pulled me into the present moment, into my life as it is now.

Enormous gratitude washed over me and fired a rocket up my backside. I wanted to appreciate today. I wanted to love today. I wanted to make sure I walked down to Balmoral Beach at 7 AM every summer morning for a swim before the blazing sun rose up into the sky. I wanted to set in motion a plan to create my most fulfilling life, based upon what I loved. One day at a time, I wanted to plant seeds of love in my heart and mind about what I really wanted out of life.

Losing Mitch was a final goodbye in one sense. Physically, I knew I'd never see him again. That type of change was a huge adjustment. If I constantly perceived it in a fearful way, I knew I'd become obsessed with my wounds, using them to control social situations, to receive sympathy, and to manipulate circumstances to get the outcome I wanted. On the other hand, by grounding myself in the loop of life and knowing that I was not separate from anyone or anything else in the world, I was learning to embrace change.

I was also learning to embrace change by connecting to my own energy. I was educating myself about the fundamental life force of the universe. I was beginning to see that energy might shift and change, but it couldn't be broken. And when I understood that my own body was made up of ninety-nine percent energy and one percent matter, I woke up to the fact that I was energy in a physical container. And so, if I knew energy couldn't be broken, but that my physical body could decompose, I knew that the large majority of who I was would live on. What was the large majority of who I was? My spirit. My energetic essence that was a part of everything else. Not different. Not separate. The same.

These days, I have the opportunity to develop a new relationship with my brother on an energetic level. If I can associate an emotional label to this ever-present, unbreakable energy, it is love. To me, love is God. God is love. Love can't be broken. I am never going to lose the love in my heart for Mitch and this new opportunity offers me a chance to expand my own love and connect to Mitch in ways I never imagined. Our relationship is undergoing major change right now, and the more I embrace it, the more unbreakable it feels. It has its own momentum and strength. Like the unpredictability of life, I don't know what direction the relationship will take me, or what insights or lessons are yet to be discovered. I'm discovering a different way of seeing things that encapsulates love. It feels more real to me than my relationship with Mitch felt when he was here. If you've ever gone through a major loss, the above is a way of looking at life in its simplicity. When the mind gets involved and attaches to what you learned through conditioning, society, and the barrage of media distraction, change becomes the scariest thing on Earth.

I encourage you to be willing to see things differently, free from what you've been led to believe. Let your own life give you the proof you need. We always have a choice. We can connect with love, our energetic essence, or we can associate the natural occurrences of life with fear. We are always in constant change so why not become the change and flow with the change? If we don't resist it, there is beauty in change. We just have to learn how to see it. When we do, life becomes a dance floor. Whether you think you can dance or not, you can awaken to the beat and move with it. Each person's genuine expression of that change is pure love. I used to call myself a horrible dancer but now I know that my authentic dance is always the life of the party, just like yours.

There is no goodbye, simply a hello to something different.

LETTER 4:
TWENTY-ONE YEARS OLD

November, 2002

Dear Mitch,

You always gave great birthday presents. I have to say this one's pretty shitty by comparison, being my twenty-first and all. Couldn't you have waited around for another month? I bet I could have put a smile on that face.

I decided to have my party at the house. Mum and Dad were happy to host, even though it's been only a hazy four weeks since you did IT. That's how I refer to what happened. IT. You did IT and IT happened. I can't bring myself to voice it in any other way. It's much easier like this. I understand why suicide is such a taboo subject, why people have trouble spitting the word out. It's like nails on a chalkboard. Why can't we open up about suicide and death and the nature of our spirits in general? Even among family and friends, it seems unnatural. What kind of programming did we have? Was *The Matrix* a movie or a documentary?

I wish I understood more about where you went when you floated off. Now wouldn't be a bad time for me to reconnect with God. Who and what is God to me? That's probably a better starting point. Maybe He has a few answers. I was never consciously close to a Higher Power in my teens, besides staring up at that giant stained glass window with all the prophets and saints in St. Aloysius' chapel. During school years of boring weekly mass, long-winded sermons, out of tune singing of hymns, reconciliation sessions, and smoky benediction services, I wish I'd been more present with the Man upstairs.

Jesus seemed like a cool guy but I always thought people misinterpreted his words and lessons. I became frustrated with the religious dogma and the guilt of committing "sin." I detached and withdrew, although I always felt a connection to something grander than our physical reality, an inner experience that directed part of my outer experience. All I had on my mind back then was – how much longer before I can bust out of here and feel a basketball in my hands? Right now, I'd like to speak with the Head Honcho. Maybe He can shed some light on this whole steaming pile of…

Our family still looks lost. Our brave faces are put to the test each day when we're out together in public. Going out in public is frightening. Yes, I have to leave the house now. I can't hide forever. But I see random people from around the area, like the cleaner, and they'll want to stop and chat and tell me how sorry they are. I appreciate that, but right now I can't handle it. None of it. The word has spread around various circles and the spotlight's on me everywhere I turn. At least, that's how it feels. That's the fear I'm living with.

Really, I'm just scared and angry. Why couldn't you have been hit by a car or eaten by a shark? Yeah, some big fat hungry twelve foot White Pointer shaped like a military torpedo with a disgracefully humongous mouth full of jagged teeth that ripped you in half, waist deep at the beach. You would have felt the initial steam train hit. Then you would have slipped into severe shock at the sight of the other half of your body floating next to some kid on his boogie board before you passed out. It would have been a tragic freak accident that no one could have done anything about. Why couldn't that have happened? At least you would have made the six o'clock news. Sorry, I'm losing my marbles here. I feel like I'm a bee's dick away from insanity. Suicide – so gut wrenching. Any other way. Please!

Looking a family member in the eye hasn't gotten any easier. Why is it so difficult? Is it because we have no idea how to confront our own mortality? Or is it the shame, the guilt, and the utter helplessness? Just how ill-prepared for death are we as a society, or as a family? It's that and at the same time, it's more than that. I look at everyone else in the house and I see my reflection. It ain't pretty. I look at Matt and Morg. When will the despair in their eyes wash away? There's the reflection again. Hopefully, it's not permanent. Otherwise, I'm tracking you down when it's my time to go. I'd like to drag you to the edge of hell, hold you over the fire and let you feel the burn. But then, I'm pretty sure you experienced some kind of living hell those last eight years on earth. Oddly, I sense your death is revealing a deeper level of understanding, like I'm a step closer to the truth – whatever that means for me. I feel it. I just can't express it the way I want to. Perhaps I don't need to express it as long as I can feel it.

It's all still so raw and I'm letting my body do whatever it needs to adjust. I have these twisted emotions that switch at a drop of a hat. It feels like I'm in a washing machine on a heavy spin cycle that doesn't want to finish. I'm still waiting for the BING! Someone, please open the door, lay me down in a laundry basket, carry me to the backyard, and hang me out to dry in the blazing Australian sun.

The birthday party is actually a welcome distraction, my chance to escape this death nightmare for the evening. My close mates have been nothing short of amazing. Most of them have no clue how to talk to me about it, including the missus. But that's okay. Their presence speaks volumes. It's louder than the music in the bar, which we rolled into sometime after 11 PM. Around that time, I took MDMA and sat down on a lounge with a few of my close mates. I'd taken the drug a few times before and enjoyed the experience, usually with my shirt off and my head against a speaker at a club. I'd never taken advantage of a contemplative conversation that was available on MDMA. This time, however, was different for the obvious reason that you'd passed on and my mind was tweaking with so many questions. While I was wrapped in a blanket of shock over the past few weeks, the eye of my mind was opening up to new possibilities.

In the afternoons when I walk down to the beach and sit on the island rocks looking out at the ocean, I feel you being carried on the ocean breeze. In these still, private moments, I can feel a new state of awareness, like I don't have to do anything, or become anyone. I forget about successes and failures and walls of limited experience. I can sit and simply be, and notice my thoughts coming and going. You once gave me a temporary taste of inner-peace on those rocks. If I can feel you even though you're not here, then do we ever really die?

The strength of my psychedelic experience in the bar shot me out of a cannon to the moon. Grief melted away in the intoxication of love. Goodbye sadness. Goodbye anger. Goodbye guilt. Hello, explosion of love. It occurred to me that my fear was all about an absence of love. And now, love beamed out of me like rays from the sun, directed at everyone and everything, including the glass in my hand. It was all-consuming, like a giant hug from God. An unveiling of a completely new level of consciousness threw me down the rabbit hole and into my own inner landscape. I was in full bloom and still expanding. I was in the confines of a bar, and yet I was boundless and connected. It was the closest I'd ever been to heaven. I felt at home in my life.

I remember sitting with my friends and falling in love with their faces. I had no concern or heaviness about your passing. The lack of fear was excellent. I was unconcerned about being in the spotlight. I didn't care what anyone thought of me. I was free to love others as deeply and unconditionally as I wanted. It was so present, so clear, so boundless as I shot out beams of loving intention towards my friends and those with whom I shared random conversations. I wanted to make a public service announcement that I genuinely wanted everyone on the Earth to be happy. My mind was blown. Life could be as deep or as shallow as I wanted to play it. It was my choice to live in this zone and I was connected to a love and a deep faith that felt visionary.

I recall thinking, *I will always be in the presence of my elder brother!* There you were, walking with me. I knew I was safe and guided. Yes! The drugs were talking. There was the potential for an awesome experience. So if it was possible on drugs, I had to know if the same experience could be replicated in a normal, balanced life without the destructive comedown of drugs. Days after I took the drugs, I would get highly emotional for no apparent reason, like while I was watching Michael Jordan *Gatorade* ads on TV.

I am not condoning the use of drugs here. They come with caveats, Mitch, as you can appreciate because you're the one who introduced me to them. Remember? Why were you such a bad role model? Why did I feel okay trying drugs with you, even after school sometimes? I wanted to do whatever my big brother was doing, that's why. I looked up to you. All those lectures from Mum about "saying no" went in one ear and out the other. It wasn't her fault. She raised us like a sensible, loving mother would. But I wanted to do what my big brother was doing. I wanted to belong with you. I wanted you here on all my birthdays.

Those exhilarating, contemplative, drug-induced hours of escape from your death came and went like a flash. Imagine that kind of love all day, every day. I have to say it'll be weird celebrating your birthday from now on. Shoot, I wonder in ten years time if I'll even remember on which day you were born in February? I have the memory of a goldfish with birthdays, except my own. I can be selfish like that – kinda like you sometimes, huh?

I'm twenty-one now. Big boy pants and everything. I do have one last question though before I turn off the lights. Did I ever really know you? And why do I get the feeling that you're about to reveal yourself?

Cheers and beers,

Marsh

MITCH TEACHES ME TO LOVE MY CHILDHOOD

IT WAS THE excessive 1980s in Sydney, when each day in our waterfront multi-million dollar home seemed like endless summer. The sky was always blue. The golden sparkle on the water was like heaven on earth. We boys had been named Matthew, Mitchell, Marshall, and Morgan. God only knew what my parents were thinking. We would swim in the pool, fish off the jetty, and zoom around the harbor in mini-speedboats and jet skis. Life was great.

One afternoon, I recall sitting on the jetty waiting for Mitch to arrive back in his boat. I saw him out on the harbor from the balcony up at the house and rushed down the two-tiered backyard steps to the jetty. As the boat approached, I saw Mitch like I'll always remember him, with beautiful wavy blonde locks, deep blue eyes, and a big bright smile on his angelic face. Loving light surrounded him. I was in awe of my brother who shone like the sun. It was as if time stopped when I looked at him and I felt a connection through the beating of my heart. I could feel something powerful that bound us, but I was too young to fully understand it.

Then, in the early nineties, the sky turned gray. The water lost its shimmer. Australia slumped into a recession as the bank repossessed houses, cars, and pubs. They took everything we had, except each other. It was around that time that Mitch's light began to dim. It was a test of faith for him. He felt exposed in the unknown of what lay ahead. I believe he had come to identify who he was with what he had. Instead of using his present circumstances as an opportunity to grow closer to the truth, he shrunk in on himself, clutching to the past.

As he grew into adulthood, with the help of drugs and alcohol, darkness cast a shadow within him where the light had been. No matter how much love we sent his way, no matter how hard we tried to help him, he chose defeat.

Today, whenever I'm standing by the shore with the water at my feet and looking out to sea, I can still see Mitch smiling, bringing his boat back home. That's where he lives in my heart.

LETTER 5:

THE FIRST SIGN

December, 2002

Dear Mitch,

Morg isn't sleeping much. Actually, he isn't sleeping at all. Thank God he didn't join us to view your body at the morgue. Morg at the morgue. Yeah, it doesn't blow kisses to begin with, let alone having that image stuck in your head. I'm not sure what he sees when he closes his eyes that keeps him awake. But I have a feeling. On your last night, he said you'd called him while he was out drinking with his buddies. You asked him to meet you wherever he was – North Sydney, I think. There you met on a street corner. These were the last moments between the two of you and they were brief. You assured him, your best friend, that you would be home tomorrow. You hugged him, got back in the taxi, and took off into the night. There was no goodbye to Mum, Dad, or the rest of us, but for Morgan, you would have done anything. Well, almost anything. Saving yourself could have been your greatest achievement.

I have some difficulty relegating the image of you at the morgue to the back of my mind. I believe that last hug and comforting words of, "I'll be home tomorrow," haunt my little brother, Morgan. Beyond the heavy sadness, he must also be feeling the same guilt we all feel. If only. Why didn't I? I should have. I can't believe I didn't. Oh fuck. Blame, blame, blame. This is the shit I'm talking about.

You're a cryptic, calculated bastard aren't you? I want to repeat those words to you again – I'll be home tomorrow. When I stared at your dead smile at the morgue, I saw you in a different home from ours. You weren't under the roof with us around a table, decked out with Mum's delectable home cooking. You were above the roof, looking down on us eating, while the spare seat at the table was collecting dust. That was what you meant, wasn't it? Wasn't it? Are you talking about an eternal home? You didn't feel at home here, did you? I want you to know that we can't and won't ever replace the spare seat at this table. Six seats make us whole. Five seats feel like a hole and our wound is visible in our eyes and in our words.

Conversation has slowed at the table, as we try to direct it to happier current events. We all took the broom out of the closet and swept the house, each room and every corner, collecting the uncried tears, the apprehensive conversations, the frightened heart revelations, the untold memories, the crystal ball predictions, the big fat elephant, and his roaring trunk. It has all been swept under the Persian rug beneath the glass dinner table.

There's a truckload under this rug and we can feel every bump. It's no wonder we're all at sea in a heavy swell, bobbing up and down, gripping the chair armrests. One more thing stuffed under this rug and it's family overboard! Did anyone pack lifejackets? Mitch, if we eventually fall into the ocean, you know we're swimming with stinky fish. It's the same stinky fish that embodies your death that sits in the middle of the dining room table every night. We hold our noses and go around it for the juicy red meats, the belly-filling starches, the creamy pastas, and the devilish sweets for dessert. Ooh baby, pain at the table never tasted so good. I hope the sleepless nights pass for Morg soon. He needs the rest. I'll always get my eight hours beauty sleep, probably eleven or twelve if there's a fat blaze involved.

You cut me short last night though, didn't you? Kept me wide-awake, the beat of my heart pulsing in the extremities of my toes and the back of my eyeballs. That feeling was bizarre but it let me know I was alive. After your visit, I sat up, flicked on the lamp and looked at my hands, front and back. I rubbed them together as if I were feeling my flesh for the first time. I swallowed, I blinked my eyes, wiggled my toes, and bent my knees. I wanted to ground myself back into reality, my real life. What happened wasn't real – was it?

It was unlike any dream I'd had before and I wondered if I was going crazy. Everything was so intensely sensorial and yet I could move beyond that to my finer self. I recall great visual clarity, like the latest in TV technology. Every color was bursting with brightness. It was exhilarating to have the overpowering feeling that there was so much more than I could ever imagine. I couldn't have dreamed what I was seeing and feeling. The air I breathed was fresher than the mountaintops. The smells were intoxicatingly blissful. There was no weight, just a lightness, an ease, but with that came strength. It was a dream, right? Dream or visitation? It scares the living shit out of me. I sense a truth, a realness behind the veil of my senses. I'm speaking to you because beyond the story and sequence of events to this dream, knowledge and wisdom were imparted to me. Where from exactly? For my own sanity, let me recall your visit.

There was a deep blue body of water, a glistening ocean that lay between two land masses. On one side of the land was the biggest crane I've ever seen at the water's edge. It rose hundreds and hundreds of feet into the air, kissing the spattering of clouds above. There you were at the very top of the crane, dangling in the air by an arm. Your hand was gripped to a metal bar and your grip was loosening. It was far away but I could see exactly what was happening. You had a nonchalant expression on your face as if you wouldn't have wanted to be anywhere else.

From the base of the crane, my instincts kicked in. I felt I had to race to the top of the crane as fast as I could to save you from falling. The climax of the movie was suddenly upon me. I climbed like a scared, frantic spider all the way to the top. You were still hanging, your body swinging gently in the breeze, back and forth like a baby's lullaby. Balancing at the top was nearly impossible. With all the strength and force I could muster, I managed to secure myself as I extended an arm toward you. My arm was there for you. All you had to do was reach. Try. Sweat dripped from my face. Just reach.

I began to yell and scream at you, "MITCH! Take my hand! I'll save you! Just take my hand! Please!"

You refused. I reached down and grabbed your arm that was holding onto the crane. I had you! It was tough to maintain my grip. I was slipping and so were you. I screamed again, "Come on, please! Take my hand, Mitch! Reach, brother!"

You weren't talking back to me, but I could hear you speak. I looked deep into your eyes that were bluer than the ocean, and I heard you say, "Let me go. There is nothing to be afraid of. Let me go. I'm fine. Everything is okay. Everything is and always will be okay."

I lost my hold on you and you fell. You ascended in slow motion and smiled at me and then you waved. You kept waving and smiling until you reached the water. There was no splash. You just blended in and morphed with the ocean. Then you were gone.

I woke up to the beat of my heart pulsing throughout my body. But there was also a soothing wave of tranquility. I didn't want to feel tranquil. I wanted to fight it and I did. Did you want to get out of here all along? Is that why you are at such peace and ease now? I would have shat my pants hanging from that crane. It was bad enough that you made me climb the bloody thing! I know you're okay, but what about us? Are we really going to be okay? I appreciate the visit. I just don't know if I believe you.

I let you slip. We all did. I wasn't ready to let you go.

Marsh

MITCH TEACHES ME TO LET GO

I SUGGEST YOU pay attention to your dreams. Pay special attention to the vivid ones where it's hard to tell between a dream state or reality as you know it. I say this because my dream about Mitch was symbolic on many levels and it held great significance in my spiritual awakening. At the time, I resisted what the dream was trying to tell me. Looking back now, though, it's as clear as day.

The significance of Mitch gracefully dropping into the ocean was his merging back to source energy, like a final awakening. The ocean represented the energetic whole and he was a single drop that made up a part of the whole, like every other drop. There was no resistance, no great splash, no broken bones, no yelling, and no screaming. It was the smoothest transition I've ever witnessed. It was effortless. I was the one yelling and screaming, sweating, and straining, doing everything in my will to save my brother from what I perceived as plummeting to his death. But it was nothing of the sort. All I saw was a smiling face and a happy wave goodbye, as if he were saying, "I'll see you when you get here." Now he could enjoy himself. He wasn't clinging to his pain or trying to push it away. He had returned to natural flow, an experience he'd struggled to achieve when he was in his physical body.

We come into this world kicking and screaming with clenched fists. We leave this world with open, relaxed palms. Mitch's relaxed, open-handed wave as he fell was symbolic of a resting transition, the evolution of another thread in the tapestry of the cosmos. There was no need for me to worry about him. He was fine. I saw it first in the mortuary when I viewed his body and noticed his peaceful smile. Then in the dream, there was that smile again. He never came to me to tell me that he was sorry for what he did. I'm sure he never intended to hurt us. But I believe he came to me to teach me something far more valuable. He came to teach me why I need to let go, not just of his hand. With his open palm, he was showing me that life opens to you when you remain open to life. Staying open means you are available to receive more of what life presents moment to moment. To remain closed is the other option, but that limits your experience. Staying shut down produces energy blocks that give rise to agitation, unrest, frustration, anger, and the collection of fearful thoughts.

In a way, Mitch was teaching me about the heart, which is our centerpiece and masterpiece. The beauty of an open heart is that we can fall in love. Energy is free to focus, distribute, and flow. When we shut down, the love stops and so do inspiration and creativity. The heart's electric, powerful capacity to produce vibrations that create and feed us cannot operate when we are closed down. When people choose suicide, the heart valve is closed. Pain and misery are pumping through the body, but not love. And with that comes desperation, as if we're struggling for clean air. The clean air Mitch needed was love. He had starved himself of love so it didn't matter what was coming towards him. He was closed to himself and everyone else.

Suicide loss places you in a tricky situation with your heart. On the one hand, you miss that precious soul with all your heart and want to snap your fingers and have him or her back with you. On the other hand, it feels like a smack in the face. You want to shut down completely and for many people, that's what happens.

I feel certain now that Mitch came to me to make sure I didn't close down after his death. Yeah, at first, I closed down alright. I was pretty good at disobeying orders and learning the hard way during my twenties. The silver lining however, is that it led me here to writing this book. I encourage you to learn to let go in every moment, no matter what life throws at you. Do you best to stay open. Like Mitch said, "There's nothing to be afraid of. Everything is and always will be okay."

I wish he'd had access to his own good advice in the first place. As I get older and expand my awareness, I believe him. It's hard to see it in the moment, but you just have to make a decision to see things differently from what you've been led to believe about death and grief.

LETTER 6:

TWO WITH ONE BULLET

January, 2003

Dear Mitch,

I'm at thirty thousand feet peering down at a platform of magical, fluffy white clouds that stretches out to the horizon. I'm having difficulty embracing and enjoying this symbolism of heaven. I'm coming down again like a ton of bricks and I'm convinced the plane is going to crash. I've also convinced myself that MDMA isn't the way forward for my spiritual quest. There has to be another way to tune in. The sky beneath me is so still, so calm, so perfect, in contrast to me. I'm a fizzing body of emotional soda ready to pop and spray all over the cabin. The stewardess keeps passing me in the aisle and asking, "Are you okay, sir?"

Very far from it, my dear. Fellow passengers are lucky I'm a master at bottling up my emotions. God knows what the scene would look like if I did finally burst open. Back up!! Where are you when I need you, Mitch?

I decided to go to South Africa and Zimbabwe for six weeks with Elle and her family. They are from South Africa and I knew this would be a once in a lifetime opportunity to enjoy the insider's track. I needed to learn to escape without the use of psychedelics. I was surprised and blessed to know Mum and Dad weren't worried about me leaving them. I can't even begin to imagine what thoughts are running through their minds. They are looking so hard at themselves right now, searching for answers that aren't there and never will be. Two beautiful people who love each other and their family with every rudiment of their being, looking one other in the eye without a word, breathing a silence that's filled with trauma: Our son is gone, our son is gone.

They breathe that into their lungs, breath after breath. How can they possibly exhale that air? I suffocate every time I go there. They have always been two giant pillars of strength in our lives. To see them shatter to pieces breaks my heart. They have always trusted me and I think they see more in me than I do at times. I love them for that.

Leaving Matt and Morg over Christmas will be hard, too. I know they need me. I wish I could show them the happy face they so desperately need. I'll do my best to bring them back something resembling that face. In the meantime, talk to me, Mitch, and steady my wings. Show me the right path to walk. I'm knocking on the door. I want out of the basement where I feel like I'm hiding. Show me a new home.

Death is following me at the moment. Johannesburg isn't what you'd call my cup of tea. Ordinary freedoms we take for granted in Australia are dangerous propositions over here. We spend three nights with the Elle's cousin, Nick, a big friendly giant with shoulders like a bull. His place is part of a complex with armed guards holding semi automatic rifles, which is part of living in Joburg. The property is electrically fenced. The windowsill in our room has an ominous line of razor sharp spikes and the upstairs is separated from the downstairs by a locked gate at the base of the bottom level of stairs. We are given pistols and told to put them under our pillows in case of intruders. Okay, I'm kidding about the pistols, but that's what I feel like Nick should be handing me before I go to bed. He gives me a joint instead, which only escalates my home invasion paranoia.

Death follows me on the roads. No seat belts. People sit in overcrowded trucks, buses, and cars driving 140 km per hour as if they're speeding away from an erupting volcano. One slip or swerve, and I think I'll be joining you on the other side. No stopping at red lights after dark for fear of a stray bullet or a car jacking. At parking garages, attendants inspect the trunk of the car. It's just a regular explosives check, they explain, no biggie. At a lunch spot, an armed guard sits in a tower perched above the car park, keeping a watchful eye on any thieves willing to roll the dice. Then of course there's the partying, or *jol* as they call it. For a couple of nights we drink at clubs until the sun comes up, only to pop straight behind the wheel and drive home. I can't walk in a straight line let alone steer a car in the dark. But hey, T.I.A. This Is Africa. At a time when I'm being shown the fragility of life, why do I put myself in potentially harmful scenarios? Please say you're watching over me.

Death continues to follow me into Zimbabwe, even amidst the raw beauty and romance of this wonderful country. I feel death swimming along Lake Cariba during two incredible weeks I spend on a houseboat. I feel like you've been shoving it in my face Mitch. I'm struggling to comprehend what you're telling me, but Jesus, slow down brother. All of this is spinning me out. Just yesterday we were fishing off a small barge, soaking up the rays, kicking back, and in bewilderment at the elephants cruising along the rocky banks. Fish eagles were perched on top of tree stumps sticking out of the water. Big piggies of Africa, the hippos, let out their deep oinky groans as they swished around in the shallows, opened their mouths wide every now and then to reveal a set of chompers that could slice you in two. Then there were the crocodiles, our sneaky prehistoric friends that lay stealth in the water, waiting for any opportunity to snap up a stray arm or leg that happened to reach down into the water, which is so very tempting in the summer heat.

So there we were fishing, Elle, her family and local Zim friends, when one of the boys, Luke, thought it would be a great idea to catch the attention of a fish eagle. He'd caught a Bream and he waved the dead fish in the air above his head trying to grab the attention of the observant flyer. Once he had piqued the eagle's interest, he decided to hook the Bream to his rod and cast out a line for the eagle to fetch off the water's surface. The eagle left his perch and circled above the fish before deciding to swoop and capture the fish with its open claws, ready to snatch a meal. Like poetry in motion, the eagle collected the fish along with the line too! The rod let out a whizzing sound as the line fizzed out of the reel at a million miles an hour.

Afraid he lost his rod, Luke yanked the line, jerking the eagle to drop the fish from its claws. I was scrambling for my camera, trying to snap whatever action I could, when the fish splash-landed down beside the boat. In my mind, I saw a flash – a huge saltwater crocodile lurched from beneath the surface without warning, right beside the barge, to grab the fish appetizer. Then he disappeared as quickly as he had sprung, without a ripple. That sly creature of the sea had been right next to us the whole time, waiting for one little screw up, one little mistake where a body part played in the water, hoping to go MUNCH! Thank you very much. Needless to say at that point, I snapped back to reality, only to see crocodiles a hundred yards away on the banks resting like statues in the sun. I was hallucinating about death.

That night, death in the form of a huge storm poured down from the heavens. A message was sent on the radio that ominous weather was approaching and we should just sit tight and prepare for the hit. It hit really hard. As Forrest Gump would say "big old fat rain" teemed, howling wind shook the boat around its anchor, testing the ropes that we had tied onto trees close to the banks. A heavy swell from the lake bashed against the sides of the boat, while booming thunder and a spectacular lightning display scared the hell out of us. I prayed to you to keep me safe, Mitch, but unlike the island rocks back home, I didn't feel your warm presence.

It's a few days later, and after a gorgeous stroll past Victoria Falls, the largest sheet of falling water in the world, we have decided to go white water rafting down the mighty Zambezi River. I'm psyched to be heading down the Zambezi with our tour guide, Colgate, who has the whitest teeth I've ever seen. We trek down a gorge to get to the water where our rafts are waiting, along with a load of crocodiles. But they are the least of our worries. We battle the sheer force of the rapids as we scale some serious Class IV and V violent currents.

The ten-person raft that I share with Elle and her brother, Scott, manages to endure what the Slambezi throws at us, not tipping so far. But, when we reach the most difficult and steepest gradient rapid that looks like a small natural disaster, we experience the full wrath of the Zambezi. Our raft flips, tossing us overboard, causing us to thrash around in the underwater washing machine. We are instructed to remain calm, pop up for air, and go with the current, making sure we don't try to stand up so we don't get our feet wedged between two rocks. I keep getting caught underneath the raft every time I attempt to come up for air. Not once, not twice, but three times I come up, struggling to find my way out from under the raft. On the third attempt I'm in a panic, even though I'm a strong swimmer. But by the fourth attempt, thank God, I'm out of the woods, my lungs clutching onto precious air. I am helped back onto my raft and I think of you. I grin, shake my head and utter, "Where were you on that one?"

We spend New Year's Eve at the Victoria Falls Casino getting rip roaring drunk. After I spend more worthless currency than I can hold in both pockets, my underwear, my socks and my shoes, we travel to a private game reserve owned by family friends. In this jaw-dropping beautiful natural sanctuary, the highlight of our holiday, I find myself in charge of death, twice as a matter of fact.

It's a scorching hot day when the owner of the reserve, Terry, takes us hunting. We load up the buckie with some cold drinks and, of course, our rifles. I've never seen a rifle before let alone held one or used one. I'm not comfortable with the thought of hunting. I'm simply keen to explore the reserve where rhinos, lions, and leopards are roaming free. Terry mentions they are culling certain animals like giraffe and impala. When I tell him I'm not going to pick up a rifle, he says that's fine.

We soon encounter zebra, wildebeests, elephants and giraffes. There is no sign of a lion or leopard at this point. I have to pinch myself. I feel so very lucky at such an unlucky time in my life. Out there in the middle of the bush, you're with me. I can feel you on my shoulders, buzzing around like an annoying fly, which creates a raging bull within me. I honestly can't comprehend the mess you made of our family. It is at this point that I ask for the rifle. "What can I have a shot at?" I ask, bouncing along in the back of the buckie.

"If we see impala, we'll slow for a shot," Terry says.

I'm brimming with anger when a herd of impala comes into view some two hundred meters away. The buckie slows to a halt. The impala nervously looks over at us. They are very still and we know the slightest sound or movement from us will disperse the group.

"Now's your chance," whispers Terry from the driver's seat. I slowly stand up, holding the rifle as I lean over the roof of the front seat to steady my gaze. Putting the scope up to my eyes brings the impala into arm's distance. I recall Terry's words to aim for the neck. That's exactly what I do when I pulled the trigger. The rifle kicks back hard into my shoulder and the herd disperses. I hit one.

As we drive closer, I can see that I've shot two impala. Two with one bullet. The first impala has been killed instantly, but the other lies dying, bleeding from its neck. Its back legs kick spasmodically and Terry gives me a large knife to slit its throat. I can't and I nearly faint. As I watched Terry slitting the dying impala's throat, my mind flashes to you. I wanted to kill you. I blamed you for my sudden surge of anger. I'd been so swift to pick up the rifle and squeeze that trigger. So much anger gushed through my veins that I laid two innocent animals to rest. After all the thinking I'd done, all the wavering emotions, all the contemplation on the nature of life and death, I'd steered into destruction.

It isn't only the animals that feel the wrath of my anger. I can feel myself beginning to implode. It's a fluke that I don't burst like a grenade when I find out that since the impala is my first kill, I'm expected to eat his testicles that night at dinner. Now, I really want to kill you. Of course, Terry and the others are playing a game on me, but I go through with the ritual. Those testes don't taste too bad on the BBQ to be honest, kind of like the fat from a juicy piece of steak. A thousand beers later around the campfire, I actually ask for more.

The next night before I go to sleep, I stand outside in the open African air and gaze up at the night sky that is sprinkled with stars. Part of me is proud to have thrilled Elle with my natural bushman skills. Another part of me is deeply sad to have killed a couple of innocent animals. For someone that's gentle, I was shocked by my own pulsing anger in the moment. Another part of me *is* upset that death *is* featured so prominently in the aftermath of your passing. It's as if it will never go away. Is death going to beat down my door any day now? God only knows.

I better have more control of my emotions these days and direct them into something positive and constructive. I can see the power of destructive patterns by looking at the results. If I can reverse that ability, if I can create rather than destruct, I can only imagine what I could achieve. There's no limit.

When I saw those dead animals, I saw your death, my own, and the death of my relationship with Elle. It was like two sides of the same coin were fighting for dominance within me – my shadow and my light. The light didn't want to be ignored and the shadow wanted to reign. I didn't love what I was seeing. Those poor animals had been in my firing line and so was Elle and anyone close to me. I felt a tug of war and I understood that exploration into my inner landscape would be the most challenging aspect of my life.

We are three-dimensional characters and we all have a shadow. You never fessed up and owned that side, sadly comfortable in your own sludge. In order to live from the light and let it shine through us, must we accept our shadow? Do we go into the shadow, acknowledge its existence within us and bless the significance it holds in our lives and the lessons it can teach us about ourselves?

All this must look like an interesting game to you now, huh? Watching us figure it all out. I better get a grip on this before it gets a grip on me.

Thanks for watching over us in Africa,

Marsh

REFLECTION:
MITCH TEACHES ME TO PLAY

WHEN I WAS very young, Mitch and I used to play in the sandpit at the side of the house in Mum's garden, surrounded by beautiful flowers and plants. We filled a huge green plastic turtle shell with sand and Mitch would help me build sandcastles with my bucket and spade. Laughing, giggling, smiling, playing. It was so simple, so fun, so pure, so present, and so innocent. Those moments were filled with light, a sense of eternity, and brotherly love.

Many years later, Mitch quoted the opening stanza of William Blake's "Auguries of Innocence" in his school yearbook. Written under his statement about what he'd like to do in the future, he quoted:

To see a world in a grain of sand
And a heaven in a wild flower,
Hold infinity in the palm of your hand,
And eternity in an hour.

I often recall this poem and reflect on our time in the sandpit. Mitch was a sensitive boy who could see an entire world in that sand. We were surrounded by Mum's heavenly garden and when he held my little hand, I could feel the whole world. We shared a timeless eternity there and to this day, when I think of that poem and the sandpit, I take a breath. I'm so grateful for the time we had Mitch in our family. More than ever, I know all he ever did was come from love.

LETTER 7:

I DON'T CARE

December, 2003

Dear Mitch,

I've been self-medicating frequently for the last six months. As a result, I don't care. I don't care. I really don't. This has become my answer to any question posed to me. I literally don't care. For a split second, this response quiets my mind from the judgmental, critical voice in my head and that's enough. If I can say I don't care countless times each day, great! This way, I can drown out the voice completely and lose it somewhere in a combo of pot, alcohol, and MDMA.

Try me. Ask me a question and before you've attached your question mark – I don't care. It's a mantra more automatic than a knee jerk reaction. I become frustrated at the drop of a hat these days. I snap at people I love and care about. I'm on edge about small things that would normally roll off my shoulders. I'm wasting time. Jesus, I'm wasting so much time. I can't focus on any one thing for longer than a few minutes. No wonder I can't complete my university assignments that don't score higher than a pass.

This final year at school I've made it almost impossible for myself. I really don't care. I'm here, I'm there, I'm up, I'm down, I'm backwards, I'm forwards. I'm never still, internally I mean. I've been still on a couch for up to four hours at a time, stoned out of my gourd. But I'm never present. My eyes dart all over the place when I talk to people. Focus! I can't focus. I'm making up stories in my head and running with them, giving them fuel, giving them fire. Of course they're based on fiction! But what do I do? I convince myself that they're true and I create a giant mess around me.

I keep rubbing my face with my hands and biting the crap out of my nails. Fuck it, I don't care. Everyone knows me as the mellow man and I'm doing my best to remain that way. I think I'm starting to resent you, Mitch. My rational mind knows I can't blame you, but I'm ready to throttle you. I'm angry and then I feel guilty that I'm angry, which makes me even angrier. Let me ask you – what did you care about? Me or anyone else in this family? Did you have any idea this would be the result of your cowardly actions – your family walking around and going mental?

I ended my relationship with Elle. I had too much anger and resentment pointed in her direction. I was fed up with… I'm not exactly sure. It was some made up story in my head. She never did anything wrong. I just came from an idiotic place. Probably the same idiotic place from which my new favorite sentence spews – I don't care. I hear the words come out and I know it hurts me a little more each time. I can't speak for everyone else in this family right now but my suffering is a peak experience. That's what feels real and so devilishly good right now.

How can pain be a good feeling? I think you know what I'm talking about, don't you? I'm identifying with this suffering and latching onto its pull, thinking I'm shielded from harm's way. But deep down in my soul, I know better. In my brief moments of insight and positive response to your passing (they come for a moment when I'm driving in my car with the radio off), I know intuitively what is true. My negativity is from years of a particular way of thinking. Everything in my experience to date has created a wall, a shield, a barrier to my truth and the beating of my heart. My heart needs to mend so my wounds will stop distorting the messages. I don't care, I don't care, I don't care.

Telling myself I don't care makes me feel arrogant and ignorant. When I said it to Mum the other day, she grabbed me by the arm and said, "If I hear those words come out your mouth once more, God help me I'll…"

She should have whacked me with a hammer. I was disrespectfully dismissing her question without consideration, and acting without love, without care, without concern for anyone but myself. Why are human beings capable of acting like that? Why do we choose to suffer? I'm starting to empathize with you, Mitch. Identifying with stories that pollute our minds poisons the roots of our tree. There is so much love in the world if we choose to see it. *If we choose to see it.*

I dropped love on the floor and couldn't be bothered to pick it up. I see myself in this moment and see myself in you – the self-loathing, the separation, the unwillingness to connect. My darker side and my big, fat ego kept telling me it's okay to behave this way. I pray that this fear is coming to the surface now in order to flush it down the toilet. I want to make way for love instead of misguided trains of thought. I know I have the choice. I know I have free will. Mitch or God or any of you angels up there, can you hear me? I'm asking to be reunited with love. I'm asking for compassion, a return to light, for God to grant me a miracle and a clear path to inner freedom, peace and tranquility. Can I get an Amen?!

I do care, Mitch. I always did. You might not have always known it, so let these words on the page help you hear it. Be my beacon of light on this journey from head to heart. I need it and so does the world.

Help me out.

Marsh

MITCH TEACHES ME TO BE AWARE OF MY THOUGHTS

I FOUND IT difficult to control my thoughts, once I'd made the decision to identify with my pain. It had been strangely comfortable to sit in my own muddy sludge. That way, I could deflect anything or anyone that opposed me. I'd just throw mud on them or on the situation. This type of mentality fuelled isolation and separation from myself and others. I could subtly feel that I was moving away from my core. I didn't want to acknowledge it, though, because that would require a lesson. I didn't want any more lessons. I was out of control, running away with swirling thoughts of destruction, living in fear.

Fear prompted me to strike out with sharp, incisive remarks and comments. Anger and violence were in my thoughts. I had a resistance to life and great confusion hit me as a result of Mitch's passing. I was terrified on the inside and the only way I knew to extinguish the terror was to numb the pain. Escape became an habitual reaction to get comfortable and my thoughts became neurotic. I didn't want to ask for help. I didn't believe in help. Who and what could possibly fix my situation?

I learned later that what we focus on expands. I focused on running away from fearful thoughts, not sitting with them and understanding them. My heightened sense of panic was trying to tell me something but only now can I see what it was. I have learned that there is value in understanding fear and how you perceive a situation. My fear was trying to wake me up to my own goodness. It was letting me know just how far I had drifted away from myself. Fear was signaling me to come back to love, even though Mitch was gone. In the dream, he'd instructed me to let go, and now, the quality of my thoughts were like alarm bells, directing me to stand up and take notice. Easier said than done, I know.

This is why I'm telling my story. We always have a choice to do whatever suits us, but we have to ask ourselves: Is this choice coming from love or fear? In my case, the absence of love was immense. My storyline was fuelling my negative thoughts, which were not serving my best interests. My grip was so tight, my heart and mind became closed, I couldn't sit with myself and be in the present moment because my habitual thoughts were running the show. While I was being harsh and unkind to myself, my fear was asking me to be gentle. Instead of going in the direction of aggression and blame, it was reminding me that there was another alternative at hand, but it required bravery. I didn't understand at the time that fear was the spearhead for courage and wisdom. My heart and mind were closed in fear, going against my natural state to stay open. Life is wide open from moment to moment, but when we are squashed or squeezed by personal challenges, we need guidance about what to do and how to be more aware of our thoughts.

I've learned that I have to work with challenge. It requires thoughtfulness to be tender with myself in times of suffering. I can't run away from fear. I need to fully experience what life is presenting me. It's a difficult learning process and I don't like the idea of becoming intimate with my pain at times. But in doing so, I strengthen my relationship with myself. I become better friends with myself. As I liberate my thoughts, I open my heart and mind. Suicide loss produces a great deal of fear, but beneath the storyline of the guilt, shame, blame and everything else, is a beautiful invitation to learn about life. It's an opportunity to stand stronger than ever before and begin to work with life, not against it. It's a chance to empower the mind to see things differently – in the warm light of gratitude.

Thoughts are things. When we're down, sooner or later we're going to hit the floor and that's an extremely painful fall. We don't have to wait for grief or our habitual thoughts to take over. We can choose to become intimate with those fearful thoughts and work with them. We simply can't change the fact of losing someone to suicide. After going to hell and back,

I know what choice I'd make if I were in the same position in the aftermath of suicide loss. I'd choose to sit with all of it and experience the intensity of what life presented and work with it – and eventually smile with it. I know it can be scary. The pain is sharp, but it's also short – far shorter than a lifetime of numbing yourself to the truth and getting lost in the stories of your mind. The human experience is varied and that includes suicide loss. To move on with your life and truly honor what you have lost, you have to change inside first. You can't change outside without first going inside.

LETTER 8:

THE VOICE NOT IN MY HEAD

December 2004

Dear Mitch,

Everyone is waiting for me to crack. In fact, I'm waiting for myself to crack. There are moments when I feel like I'm about to fall to bits. When that happens, I mentally slap myself across the face and steady myself with a deep breath through the nostrils. When I'm in the car, I'll hear a song, any song really, and attach a story to it about you. From there I choke. My throat literally closes up. I feel energy surging from my stomach, my heart, my being. I want to surrender to mourning you, but my mind has other plans. It sends me a message to stay strong because that's what men do. Big boys don't cry. That's how we deny ourselves love.

That message attacks my throat. I know this stage is going to catch up to me. I'm not looking forward to the rush of bottled up grief that is bound to unravel once I open up. I'm not sure I want to feel that yet. I've run from my own emotions and heavy situations in the past – out of sight out of mind. Swept under the carpet. But I can't run from this forever. I don't want to be a runner. Ironic coming from a track athlete, I know. I'm plagued by this fear of isolation and who I am at my core. An inner voice speaks to me: Trust and let go, trust and let go. I hear him speak. You're some piece of work, Mitch. You've thrown me into the depths of a psychological and emotional maze. Each time I turn a corner, I'm obstructed by a wall of that word again – fear. Let me run straight. Let me be safe. I want out. I need to take the spotlight off this brave face because you know I'm crumbling inside.

I need some advice. Why is that is so hard? And then, why am I coming to you for answers like you're some almighty oracle or sage? A guy who killed himself. A guy who didn't have any answers so he took the easy way out. The only time I asked you for advice in the past was about how to tackle on the rugby field. You were a fearless rugby player. You were never the biggest guy on the field but you were the most psychotic. I once saw you dive at a player's foot, attempting to charge down a kick. You were like a dog on a bone. In the process, a player forcefully kicked you directly in the head when you were in mid-air. You were knocked out before your head hit the ground. But you always hit hard and in the right places. You rarely missed tackles. You were the first player to every ruck, rummaging for the ball like a wild animal on a carcass. You were possessed on the rugby field, an area of life where you lived fully without hesitation or regret. Qualities I always admired.

One day, you taught me how to tackle. I was all skin and bones. A stiff breeze could have blown me over when you took me out into the living room and told me to stand still at one end. Then you backed away to the other end of the room with that cheeky grin of yours.

"Now what?" I said.

"Just stand still. I'm going to show you how it's done," you said.

"Please don't hurt me!"

"Quiet. Just watch."

Then you charged at me and tackled me like your opposite number on the field. I went crashing backwards to the floor with the wind knocked out of me. You got to your feet and stood over me with that same cheeky grin as I gasped for air.

"So," you said, "think you got it now?"

I had learned how to tackle although it was a couple of years after school was over when I learned to enforce it with strength, minus the kamikaze style.

Driving through the gates of the cemetery, my eyes well up. My heart is squashed with never-ending blame, guilt, shame, and confusion that I have no idea how to process. I see your funeral procession in a flashback and space out behind the wheel. I hear you laughing. It's the voice of a child. I park the car, making my way through the fields of the dead to your plot right next to Nan. How is the old girl? I take a seat on the mint condition grass at the base of your bronze grave plaque and look around. It's just you and me and the wind passing through the trees, carrying with it the souls of the departed. God, I feel so silly sitting here. I'm about to talk to the ground. Who's lost his noodle now? I close my eyes, settle my breath, and wait. After a few welcome moments of stillness, I feel the bag of cement sitting on my chest gently begin to lift. A warmth tingles up my arms and over my shoulders and down my spine, through my hips and out into my legs. I'm light as a feather when I began to silently talk to you. I tell you:

Something's changing. I feel a wave of energy guiding me. I feel it wherever I go, whatever I do. Is that you? I feel at ease when I allow it to flow through me. But this process isn't easy for me. I lack faith. I feel that faith requires me to be visionary and I have no vision for my life. No clue whatsoever. Maybe that's why I party so much. Where does that leave my vision of the heart? Under the rubble. I need to build a new home and allow these changes to catch fire and start a Holy flame inside me. What the hell are these changes? Why do I feel so out of control? I wouldn't mind not having it all worked out right now, but since your death, I feel pressure. Watch him be a fuck up after his brother killed himself, I can hear people say.

There goes my mind again. Is that what I want them to say? The mind is a powerful thing, isn't it? I feel like more of a slave than a master. You became a slave. You! The smartest guy in the room and look what happened to you! It turned against you. You let it beat you. Beat you down each and every day. You bought into the stories, the past, the crazy. You let it consume you and ultimately defeat you. When we water our garden with love, we watch it grow. When we water it with suffering and fear, we watch it die. All I'm asking is for a healing to occur. How do I heal myself of this fear?

I remain in silence with my eyes closed, waiting for your response. I don't hear you, Mitch. There is someone else though, which sounds unfamiliar. This voice is not coming from my mind. It's coming from the center of my being, my core. It's clear, precise, honest and assuring. Is this the real me talking?

"Trust and let go. That is all you have to do. Trust and let go."

How do I start with that? How do I drop the bags of conditioning and the past? Can I trust in you Mitch, my guardian angel? If you were standing at the edge of a cliff and someone told you to trust and let go – would you take that first step off? How does the path magically appear before me? Remember that time we saw *Indiana Jones and The Last Crusade* at the movies? Harrison Ford had to take a leap of faith in order to cross the chasm to reach the Holy Grail. I recall Sean Connery's character saying, "You must believe, boy, you must believe." That's how it feels, but this isn't the movies. This is life. My life.

If I walk the path of the voice inside – do you promise to walk with me?

Marsh

MITCH TEACHES ME TO CONNECT TO A HIGHER POWER

I WAS NEVER clear about my relationship with a Higher Power or God. I believed in a universal energy of some kind that was the essence of creation. Before Mitch died, though, I had never gone into any depth with my relationship to source energy. I hardly ever reflected that I was a part of it or connected to it. I enjoyed my solo times with Mitch at the cemetery. It was quiet and almost every time I visited, I was the only person in sight. I could tune in and listen to life. In those moments, I could feel an intelligence contained in my grief that was directing me where to go.

Why did this invitation to connect to my own energy and a Higher Power come about? Why did I feel compelled to investigate what I thought was my identity? After Mitch died, my physical body and the mental images of myself that I carried around disappeared. It happened organically. Behind my anguished mind, energy rose up from the pit of my stomach. I came to realize this energy as the essence of who I am. I was compelled to investigate because I felt I had to, in order to explore the depths of life and connect to Mitch on the spiritual plane.

In order to trust in a universal energy – let's call it a Higher Power – and openly connect to and understand my own energy, I had to identify what that meant and felt like to me. I used the process below that I learnt from spiritual leader Gabrielle Bernstein to develop my connection to a Higher Power, as I answered the following questions:

What does a Higher Power mean to me?

It means there is an invisible force far more powerful than I can imagine or comprehend. It is the architect of everything contained on Earth and the Universe. It is a loving energy that creates and heals. A Higher Power means that maybe I was put on this Earth for a reason and my job is to discover that and honor the blessings I've been given. It means I can ask for help when I need it, that there is someone looking out for me and wants me to be happy.

What does it mean to rely on a Higher Power?

It means that I am not alone on this journey. It's an opportunity to develop my relationship with a Higher Power and be open to its presence within and around me. Relying on a Higher Power means I can place my faith in the ever-present, unbreakable source that brought me here. It feels like a type of magic that is working with me when I open up to receive guidance. It means I feel stronger and more grounded – that no matter what happens, it's part of the process designed for my higher good.

What does it feel like when I'm connected to this Higher Power?

Safe. Warm. Light. Expansive. Connected. Plugged in to life. It feels like I have room to move, spaciousness within my being. Room for discovery. Room to receive. There is a platform and foundation for living without intrusion, association, or distraction. Clarity is the word I'm looking for – clarity that it's okay to just be in the present moment. Nowhere else to go. Nothing to grasp from yesterday. Being connected is pure presence and aliveness bursting with energy that I can feel pulsing through my skin. I am safe and most of all, I've been here all along – a part of life's dance, which sounds fluffy but true for me. It gives me confidence to know all I have to do is be me. Right here, right now.

How does this Higher Power relay messages to me?

Most commonly I get a "gut feeling" or physical reaction. Other times I hear an inner voice, such as when I sit at Mitch's grave in silence or in meditation. The voice is not of the mundane mind, but rather of the universal mind. This is how I understand that my Higher Power is communicating with me. Sometimes I see things – call them signs – that I can't ignore. Some people call them coincidences. I call them mini-miracles. Synchronicity in effect.

How would it feel to be in constant contact with a Higher Power?

That's easy. It would *feel* like heaven. Nirvana. To be in a place of constant contact with a Higher Power would be like living the ultimate dream, wide awake and ready to go, coach! It would be like ubiquitous fearlessness, an off-the-charts inner confidence about life. I would feel crystal clear that no matter what happens, everything is okay. I don't need to buy into the mind's neurotic thoughts and feed them. I can master the complexity of the ego and simplify my life. I can be in love 24/7 and all my relationships are endless flowing channels of giving and receiving love. Funnily enough, it reminds me of a scene in *Happy Gilmore* when Kevin Nealon's character, Potter, gives Happy some golfing advice: "You got to harness in the good energy, block out the bad. Harness, energy, block, bad. Feel the flow, Happy. Feel it. It's circular."

Most significantly, being in contact with a Higher Power would assure me that Mitch is perfectly fine and enjoying his transitory state in the spiritual realm.

What blocks my connection to a Higher Power?

Buying into my own fearful thoughts and fueling them blocks my connection to a Higher Power. When I cling to the past or feel anxious about the future, I block the connection. The speed at which modern life operates including the media distraction, being affected by people's opinions, spending time on pointless scrolling through social media feeds, keeps me disconnected. So does hanging around people who don't support my growth and who have no interest in changing. The belief that I was separate from everyone else after Mitch died blocked me. Bursts of anger, blame, guilt, and believing negative stories kept me disconnected. Essentially, when I buy into the mind and the speed at which the modern world expects us to operate, I became blocked from a Higher Power.

When do I feel most connected to it?

During meditation is when I feel the deepest and strongest connection to a Higher Power. I also feel connected to a Higher Power when I feed myself joy, plain and simple. That might be a daily swim in the ocean, a long walk through the bush, spending time with my girlfriend and close friends and family, journaling, praying, observing children and nature, enjoying a lovely meal, feeling the sun on my face or listening to music that I love. Feeling grateful for small daily delights helps me feel connected to a Higher Power.

What is my Higher Power trying to tell me when things aren't flowing?

It's usually a wake up call. An opportunity to stop, check in with myself and reassess what is happening at a particular moment. My grief, my understanding of death and how I choose to deal with it are messages from a Higher Power to shift my thinking.

During challenging times when I'm swimming upstream, I need to ask myself: Why I am doing this? Is it serving me? Is it in my best interests to continue on this path? Something is out of balance that needs subtle or obvious attention. Basically, I know that I have moved away from my true center, love, and taken a left hand turn into fear.

Higher Power Connection Affirmation

As a daily reminder – I have created a Higher Power Connection Affirmation. This confirmation of my own belief was given to me through Mitch's passing. I read it daily when I wake up and again before I go to bed at night. I notice how it feels in my body when I say the words, followed by a few minutes of reflection and gratitude:

"I am consciously awake to the universal love and intelligence that creates and heals. I trust wholeheartedly and have unconditional faith in its presence within me. When I connect to that presence and live and lead from its loving strength, I can spread my wings and fly. I can then inspire others to spread their wings and fly. I am love and love is the voice of God."

PART TWO:
CRACKING OPEN

LETTER 9:
THE POWER OF SILENCE

April, 2005

Dear Mitch,

After I somehow managed to graduate from university, I left Sydney for Japan to teach English to kids in a small town called Ichinomiya, a short distance outside the city of Nagoya. Sydney is a beautiful, bustling city. It has clean beaches, a breathtaking harbor, lovely weather, solid public transport, infrastructure, and opportunities to build a career. But it's also expensive and insular, a pre-ordained existence with boxes to tick in order to fit in and not feel judged. This kind of pressure and psychic noise are perfect conditions for the ego to flourish as people focus on property, investments and where to live. What school did you attend? What do you do? Who are you friends with? Where did you have your wedding and your honeymoon? How many kids are you planning to have?

I left for Japan because I needed to get away from my friends and my surroundings. I was ready to tune into a different channel and more than ever, you were on my mind. I wanted to know more about death, the inner workings of my being and this universe. The knowledge that there was something bigger than my physical body and the physical world drove me to investigate.

So here I am in Ichinomiya, teaching English, living in a small studio, taking another step towards healing. I can't fit on the toilet seat in my apartment. I feel like I'm living in a doll's house as I sit on an undersized chair at school with my knees touching my chin, much to the amusement of my fellow teachers. I'm sure I had this desk once when I was five. I have to duck my head four inches to fit inside the classroom doors where I'm greeted with screams from my cute little Japanese youngsters, "Here comes Sensei Freak!"

When I stand on the train, the other passengers come up to my armpits. I sleep on a mattress on the floor where my feet hang over the edge. I have no TV. I have no computer. I have no internet. I have no radio. I have no calls to answer. I have no calls to make. I have no family members' eyes to reflect the memory of you. I have next to no comprehension of this beautiful Japanese language, and I have no noise. For the first time that I can remember, *I have no noise.*

All I have is a small brown couch, a tiny balcony where I can barely extend my arms laterally in both directions, a snow-capped mountain in the distance, my busy thoughts, and this unfamiliar silence. I asked for a break but now what? Where do I start? Why on earth did I come to Japan to sit in silence and teach English to nose-picking six-year-olds? Couldn't I have gone walkabout in Australia and rented out a shack in the bush somewhere? That would have been easier, wouldn't you say? I listened to my inner voice one day at your grave. Trust and surrender was what I heard, but surrender to what? Are you still with me, Mitch?

It's Sunday morning and raining heavily. I can't see the mountain as I stand on my balcony for a moment in the cool air and gaze out at a sea of gray clouds. I inhale deeply. The words *trust* and *surrender* ring in my cluttered mind. I shoo these pearls of wisdom back to the closet. I step back inside, sit on my brown couch, and become smothered in silence. I sit still with my hands in my lap and simply breathe, feeling the rise and fall of my chest. I am still. I don't have to be anywhere or see anyone or be anyone. I can just be. I can sit and breathe deeply and fully take in my new surroundings. That's when I literally freak out. It isn't fear of being alone or out of my comfort zone. It's the fact that I'm questioning everything in my life.

Here, in a new reality, I feel a falsity about my life. I feel the real me beneath the surface and I think about the word "expression." Have I ever expressed who I am deep down? Have I ever given myself that opportunity? What do I want to express? What is my contribution to the world? Did you ever express your true self, Mitch? Was your death a final expression about what life holds for us? Was that your gift to me?

I sink a little deeper into the couch. I stare blankly out the window. The last time I asked so many questions, I was barely tying my own shoes. In a way I feel like I'm tying my life's new shoes for the first time. I watch fat drops of rain splash onto the balcony railing as the overwhelming power of your death sweeps over me. I'm tingling until my entire body begins to gently shake. I'm bubbling inside with a flood of combustible emotion. The dam of grief is overflowing and I couldn't hold the gates closed any longer.

The bubbling surges from the pit of my stomach into my heart like soldiers storming into battle. There is no clear and distinct emotion. It is everything I have. My heart carries the heavy bags of loss, sadness, grief, anger, fear, relief, and joy. When I think about us playing together in the sandpit, the gates burst open as I begin to cry. I wail, rocking forward and crouching over my knees. I cry and wail and cry and cry and cry for hours. My tears are for you, Mum, Dad, Matt, Morg, and for me. It's weird to say, but it's the most alive I've ever felt, as if I'm cracking open from a cocoon.

This outpouring and cleansing feels riddled with Holiness as a powerful energy flows through me, giving rise to something greater, something bigger. I'm being stripped down, it's a shedding, a goodbye, but not to you. I'm rinsing off the dead skin. A fresh coat of me is underneath, a rebirth. Aliveness is knocking on my door coming from a part of me I forgot about – my soul. It is making me spring into action. Even though the rain continues its steady stream, the day has taken on a new kind of potential. Aliveness is poking through my extremities and out into the world as I rise, shower, dress, eat a bowl of udon and walk out the door with an umbrella. I have no idea where I'm going, but I'm going. Aliveness is moving me forward.

I take the train to the city of Nagoya and walk through damp city streets with a spring in my step. I have no map. I'm just walking with no agenda like I'm being steered. Do you have me by the hand, Mitch? I'm on autopilot moving along these streets for the first time, pushing forward, knowing there is some place I'm destined to be. It's a peculiar and odd experience as I walk into an English bookstore. I have NEVER just happened to walk into a bookstore. A sports store, yes! A pet store, yes! A bakery, oh-my-Lord yes! A bookstore in Japan? Sorry, wait – what?

I feel like I belong on the shelves. There is a pulsing, a vibration coming off them that I can't ignore as if the books themselves are giving off their own energy. I feel them beaming into my heart that has cracked open to a new light. Why are these authors calling my name? Logical sense eludes me because inside, nothing has ever made more sense. Today's journey has taken me along an unknown path that bizarrely feels like home.

I stop at the shelf of books on mysticism, world religions, philosophy, astrology, numerology, spirituality, and self-help. The only religious or spiritual book I've ever skimmed is the Bible and that wasn't by choice. I stop at one particular title – *Synchrodestiny* by Deepak Chopra. I've never heard of Deepak or this book, but it draws me like a magnet. I pick it up and hold it in my hands. Beneath the title I read, *Harnessing the Infinite Power of Coincidence to Create Miracles.*

That's all I need. I don't read the back cover or the introduction. I have no second thoughts. My skeptical mind is quiet as a firm belief washes over me that this book is the first brick to build my new house. What this new house might look like I'm not sure, nor am I sure of its contents. That doesn't matter. What matters is that I feel light as a feather, flowing naturally, not having to do anything except enjoy the ride.

On my way to the cashier, I pass a small crafts section with paper, cardboard, picture frames, colored pencils, paints, and brushes. I've never thought of myself as an artist beyond bubble painting in pre-school or attempting to mold a mug from clay in the eighth grade. But here I am, being driven up a new path, ready to turn into a different neighborhood. I pick up six sheets of cardboard, some pens and pencils, and some glue and scissors. Strange? Very. First grade school project? Feels like one as I approach the counter where I see a pile of notebooks. I pick up seven of them and while I pay, I smile, another thing I hadn't given myself permission to do on a regular basis.

The rain has stopped when I walk outside. I have three full plastic bags in my hands and I hug my umbrella under my armpit. I don't look left or right or wonder where I am or what I'm going to do. I walk straight back toward the train station and head home in a state of bliss. Who the hell is this guy? I think. Maybe I've had too much miso soup. Marshall Dunn is riding a train in Japan with a book that he's probably going to read! And God only knows what I'm going to do with a pile of books, pens, and paper! A voice in my head tries to convince me I've drunk away any sane brain cells. It's the same negative voice that's always talking, that loves to spoil anything that feels natural at my core.

Why do I deny the things that feel natural? If the thinking mind is so natural, why is it prone to harbor unnatural behavior that makes me feel so small? I shut those thoughts down and continue on my way, smiling at Japanese strangers who pass me in the street. They smile back, hopefully somewhat genuinely, even though I'm a 6'2" white guy with eyes like dish plates showing off my big toothed grin. My senses feel heightened and I feel joyful. Is this the state of bliss that people call "presence?"

With my new purchases spread out on the floor, I park myself on the brown couch. I look out the window toward the snow-capped mountain where the clouds have begun to clear. The lightness in my body is so different from the weight of the morning. In a desire to investigate these feelings, I close my eyes and breathe in my natural rhythm. I am surprised that my mind is reasonably quiet. Normally, I hear a heavy metal rock concert of thoughts moshing around in my head. Now, I hear my heartbeat drumming through my body, loud and clear, a welcome sound.

I begin to lose feeling in my head, almost as if it has fallen off. Pretty soon, that sensation goes down the back of my spine and into my hips until I can't feel any part of my body. In this quiet space, thoughts come and go. Random positive affirmations penetrate my core, while negative thoughts vanish from my force field. Right now, nothing can harm me. I feel powerful, honest, and full of love. It feels real. Is this all-consuming force of love the key to unlocking my purpose? Is it the key to understanding death in this continuum of life? Is it the key to healing our family? Or is it simply an insight, a lesson to imprint my mind and carry in my heart about how to live life? Is it everything?

Forty minutes pass. I slowly open my eyes and land back on planet Earth. Where the hell did I just go? I pick up a notebook and a pen. I open up to the first empty page, take a deep breath, and I start writing. I feel at home in a home I've never known before. It's the best feeling I've ever had.

Over the next three months I write non-stop in the mornings before work and into the nights after work. I fill piles of notebooks with a stream of consciousness about your death, my life, your life, our family, our world. I'm spewing up everything and oddly, I feel smarter than ever. I write poems of love and joy, of fear and doubt, of sadness and anger. I recall that a tutor at school gave me a fountain pen as a parting high school gift. Maybe she saw something I didn't? I purge the depths of my darkness onto these pages and make way for clarity. It feels like a bright warm light I've seen before but didn't understand.

The more I write in this blissful silence, the more I want to investigate the silence and pleasure of writing. I figure that's the best way to speak to you, Mitch, to listen to you. From here, I teach myself how to meditate while reading multiple books from Deepak Chopra. He is a great starting point for me and for us, Mitch. He is the next catalyst, the next coincidence that urges me to contemplate the place from which you originated and where you returned. Within a matter of weeks, what started out as ten minutes in the morning and ten at night, has become forty-five minutes at sunrise and then again in the evening. I have no idea what's going on, but I'm not struggling. During these months in this silent apartment, I felt like I'm being used. I recall the Saint Francis of Assisi prayer from ten years of school mass:

Lord make me an instrument of Thy peace.

The act of writing is the instrument and the processing of my internal dialogue gives rise to inner peace. It is so weird.

My questions for you, Mitch, never stop coming. Are you actually dead? When I started the process of cleansing my grief and feeling alive and connected to an inner force, was I being led into the bookstore? Was that an indication of "something else" that exists within each and every one of us? Are you really dead? Okay, physically I can still see you dead in the morgue. But what about the guy who's showing me an inkling that something bigger exists? He's not of the mind. He can't be because I feel him in my core when he speaks to me. That guy's invisible. What about him? If I have him inside of me, just like you do and everyone else does, how can the power of that spirit die? It is so limitless, boundless, endless, and enormous, it's beyond comprehension.

It morphs into everything. It becomes everything. Is it everything? Is this real liberation, this surrendering and trusting whatever is happening without the mind making decisions, bogged down in all its complication, stories and drama? Is it all just happening? Is there actually nothing to do? Why are we striving, pushing, grasping, holding, chasing, climbing, if it doesn't feel natural? It's stressful, it's the same as everyone else, its bland. I mean, God made everyone look different for a reason. Each and every one of us has something unique and different to offer. At the same time, that special something comes from the same place that we all share collectively – LOVE.

It's love, right? Shed some light big brother, please. This Japanese BBQ and the living room just got a little intense. But am I right? Any mindset not derived from love is the creator of bullshit. Now I see why we're so distracted. We're in a vast ocean of conditioned currents pulling us into an undertow of seasoned habits and stories that don't serve anyone. We're asleep. Lifeless. I'm the result of how society, family, and school has molded me. I copy and paste a million different habitual, meaningless experiences day after day. Am I supposed to be happy with that kind of programmed meaning and lack of purpose? I guess that's our way of surviving.

How do I change my life from here? If I know what's real, help me change my life. If I can't, if the world can't, man, what kind of future do we have to look forward to? And to think, all it took was tears, a little faith, consistent meditation, inward reflection, a pen and paper, some udon, and some Japanese fried chicken from the supermarket. Who knew?

Marsh

MITCH TEACHES ME THE BENEFITS OF TIME ALONE

BLAISE PASCAL ONCE said, "All of humanity's problems stem from man's inability to sit quietly in a room alone." There has never been a truer word spoken in my opinion. Time alone with myself without distraction over the years has been a blessing, particularly my time in Japan. My grief showed up in the present moment, free of any interruptions. I gave myself permission to allow what needed healing to flow freely. Most people are terrified of silence, afraid of their own cathartic responses to inner-fears, self-doubts, and past hurts. If only we could focus on the liberation that lies on the other side! The idea of creating a silent space for healing to occur is terrifying because deep down, hearing the truth means change and disruption from the herd-like consciousness.

Silent revelations of bottled up feelings and doubts are scary for the majority of us. How do we face the truth about any number of things, from how we're currently living life to our intimate relationships, our career, our physical and mental health, our spirituality, sexuality, family relationships, and wealth. Who am I? What's my purpose? What am I grateful for? Sure, it's easier to distract yourself. But in the end, it's so much harder to walk through life numbing yourself to what longs to be heard. So much harder.

Time alone doesn't always have to be filled with dramatic revelations. It can be an inspiring, up-lifting, creative, and energetic experience. A place to question and/or affirm your focus on what you really want in life. God comes to the quiet mind. In my own experience, when I engage in a world full of intrusion and noise, I lose connection to myself. I feel confused, like I'm not enough, while I search the external world for an illusory remedy that will fix everything. Meanwhile, all the answers I'm looking for and everything I want is within me.

Time alone is a chance to sit in gratitude, reflect on what I have in my life – all the little things and whatever is yet to come. I use quiet time alone to reflect on my behavior, thoughts, and beliefs. More often than not, silent solitude is where clarity can breathe. If nothing else, I can enjoy just being with myself. No attachments to yesterday, no anxiety about tomorrow. Just where I am in the moment. Nothing else but my breath and my surroundings. I can experience the fullness of silence when I have nowhere to be, or nothing to do. I can be just me. It's a gift and it's free.

When I look at the balance of life, it makes sense to be in the midst of life and still allow time for silence away from the noise. When a personal crisis came along for me like suicide loss, life continued but I needed time alone to sit with my grief and externalize it in some capacity. My time in Japan was a beautiful combination of tears, writing, and meditation. Being alone and silent is not going to be the same for everyone. The point is that the longer we run away or neglect what longs to be heard or released, the more harmful it becomes.

For me, silence is a powerful resource to become more authentic, creative, and self-aware. It always starts with the individual. It always starts inside. Cultivate time to be alone with yourself. It will only serve you to become a happier, more self-aware, self-loving man or woman. All you need to do is start.

Take the first step in faith, said Martin Luther King, Jr. *You don't have to see the whole staircase, just take the first step.*

It's difficult to surrender to faith when you're living in fear. I can't begin to imagine the fear when someone is contemplating ending his or her life. But fear is merely potential, like everything in life. We can learn to have faith in the potential of love or in fear. You can ask anyone on the street, *Which would you prefer, love or fear?* Love will always be the answer. Yet for so many of us, the natural state of love seems unattainable. Unnatural, misaligned thoughts of fear have become the norm, and we wonder why we're so unhappy and frustrated with life.

My outpouring of grief in Japan and the glimpse of a return to love within me, allowed me to see how far I'd drifted, something that started before Mitch's death. A spark of faith returned. With faith came confidence. It was a step towards coming back to my essence and discovering what it is I truly wanted in life. In that space, life doesn't feel as daunting. Unwinding a lifetime of conditioning takes more than a day's work. But faith can shine a light forward. I saw a light shining forward in Japan. I wanted to write. I felt it was the gateway to my soul, a staircase to healing and unlocking my inner truth.

Faith took me to New York City. Faith paved the way. Faith kept me asking the right questions.

LETTER 10:

VULNERABLE IN CENTRAL PARK

October, 2005

Dear Mitch,

Was it fear that killed you? Did the inner trappings of your mind pollute the whole into submission, overpowering the light that begged you to return to its loving embrace? Were you scared of being you, your original flavor? Did you ever allow yourself to fully expand, to take a form that may have stunned people who saw you every day, who knew you the best? Did you ever hear someone else talking from your beating heart who felt only lightness, love, and peace? As you experienced each birthday, could you feel yourself drifting away? Did you feel there was a missing piece to a perfect puzzle that would allow you to live in grace on this physical plane? Did you try to extend beyond your senses to hear the calling of the angels? You just might have been able to breathe in the stillness that would have allowed you to engage in the power and magnificence that your wholeness provided.

I see you like I see any stranger or friend, the sparkle or dullness in the doorway to the soul. Your eyes speak the truth and communicate with me through inspiration. I see your fear, love, disdain, anger, frustration, peace, and tranquility. You are a pure child, and I know that your darkness was of the ego, the jealousy, the judgments that tied a noose around your neck. I see your past hurts, your future excitements and anticipations, and I feel my connection to those beautiful round eyes. I wish I could cut open your chest and expose your fear of being viewed as an outcast. I see your bare bones, the rawness of your experiences. We all wanted to see the authenticity, inspiration and selflessness of a true leader. We wanted to see your vulnerability and we wanted you to own it. I would have sat there and cried with you until there was no room for anything else to emerge other than laughter and new beginnings. You were never alone.

I wish you could sit here with me on this wooden bench in Poet's Walk in Central Park. The leaves fall gently because they know it is their turn to die. They were born and they lived in color. What more could anyone possibly ask for? A life well lived! A tree is never afraid that its leaves won't return. The tree is vulnerable and knows how to let go. It knows that the leaves will come again when the time is right. It's bizarre to look at nature and see the parallels, the lessons of life, and how to live. Humans are a complex species. When the power, trust, and unconditional love within us is fully realized, perhaps we'll have no need to wave good-bye so soon to souls like you, Mitch. You were something greater than your pain. But I wouldn't be sitting here, my new favorite place in the city, if it weren't for you.

My challenge and mission is to live these words and stop fighting with life. I've shot too many relationships in the foot before they had a chance to blossom. I've been my own worst critic. Before I join you in the eternal realm, I'm learning to be vulnerable. Maybe it will seem as beautiful as the red leaf that just landed gently on my lap.

Marsh

REFLECTION:

MITCH TEACHES ME STRENGTH IN VULNERABILITY

YOU NEVER USED to hear an emotional peep out of me. I held my cards very close to my chest. Perhaps it was conditioning from seeing Dad hold in his own self-expression. But he and I grew up in different eras. I felt that it was unnatural not to speak about matters of the heart. It made me feel like I had a weight on my chest. I never saw bottling up emotion and blocking energy as a sign of strength.

As Spirit kept ringing my bell to properly grieve and investigate what was inside me, vulnerability opened me up to a new way of thinking. It was real and honest. We all struggle to be real with ourselves and honor our own authenticity. Why are we afraid of who we really are? We're afraid of judgment, comparison or how bright we might shine, fearful of our own greatness. Mitch died without being vulnerable. He was never alone within himself or with his family. His mind spiked his tree and chopped it down. He never gave vulnerability a chance to help him heal.

The beauty and magic of vulnerability is that we discover our inner-most thoughts and feelings. We have an opportunity to cleanse and heal. Vulnerability is the path to creativity, to new ideas and revelations. With vulnerability, we have the ability and the courage to create real and lasting change because there is nowhere to hide. The truth has space to breathe and we have the chance to shed the old skin. When I chose to be vulnera-ble with myself, I also chose to face my fears. I could stay where I was and shrink, or I could take a small step and challenge myself. I could open up and see who was really inside. Mitch's death provided me the opportunity to be vulnerable for self-discovery so I could feel myself get stronger.

Life is one hell of a rollercoaster, especially after a great loss. But you can't stay numb to your emotions forever. You have to play an active role in your life, take risks, and stay true to yourself. Feeling your emotions and becoming vulnerable can carry you across the roughest seas. Over time, they become smoother because you have become grounded and rooted in your own being, in your own truth. When you are brave enough to lay it all on the line and choose not to sink in the ship of grief, you risk being seen, warts and all. But guess what? That's okay. That is genuine authenticity. That's all of you and there's nothing to be ashamed of. In my opinion, that's true strength and the beginning of living the life you were meant to live.

LETTER 11:

THE MAN WITH THE MASK

November, 2006

Dear Mitch,

Ever since you died, I lie awake at night wondering who I am. I used to go to bed fantasizing about a dream holiday, a dream woman, a dream anything that I didn't have in that moment. Who am I? I keep asking over and over again. And the more I ask the question, the more aware I am that I am not really being me.

That scares me to death. My face seems to be different for different people. It's as if I have a suitcase full of masks accompanied by matching personalities. I feel like an actor, longing to play the only role that matters, that gives meaning and purpose to my journey. Like picking the right Powerball numbers, I'm ready to cash in on the jackpot that will change everything. But why do I persist with the charade? Who were you behind your mask, Mitch? Is this the gift or curse of your death?

I am Marshall – the name given to me on November 2nd, 1981. But who is Marshall? By definition, I am a horse steward. I am your brother. I am a son to Mum and Dad, a friend, a colleague, a boyfriend. I am all these things, but I don't know who I am. Now that I'm back in Sydney, I'm falling back into old habits. Boozing hard – the Australian way. With every hangover, I move further away from myself. My body's reactions tell me the drink doesn't serve me, but I ignore the signs. When Thursday or

Friday of the following week comes around, the itch is there to do it all again. Insanity? Yes.

Then there's our bonding herb, remember? I actually don't mind a puff-puff here and there that tunes me into nature and my surroundings. Too much of it, though, and the apathetic sloth kicks in. You'll be thrilled to know that I've also discovered cocaine. Good thing it's highway robbery – something like three-fifty for a gram. I never purchase it, but I love to scam a rail off whoever is sharing their goody bag. I blame you. The day you chose to leave us was the day my mind became riddled with confusion. Pandora's box was opened and my whole existence came into question. Is this what suicide does, Mitch? It leaves a person isolated from the normalcy of life as we investigate the destruction of our lives. I beg to unravel the truth. Maybe then I can live a more honest life. I don't want to keep hiding behind these masks. When I see my truth, will I be able to see the truth of you, too? Will that truth set me free from my limited beliefs about what is possible? Will I find peace and love? Will I ever see your suicide as a gift rather than a curse?

I try not to think of your suicide as a curse. But when my mind is running a million miles an hour, I wish you were still here. Better still, I wish you were thriving, healthy, wealthy, and wildly successful in whatever you chose to do. The capacity was there. Why didn't you go in search of what you needed? All you had to do was look within. Imagine what your life and ours could have looked like. Your wife, your kids, and your house with a beautiful garden like the ones we grew up with. I see a pool with a diving board as you show me how you do forward flips. I see you well-dressed, keeping fit and limber, a great father with wisdom to impart to your children. You manage the barbeque on Sunday lunches at your house. These juicy steaks taste amazing! This would-be-life tastes amazing.

Did you ever dare to taste what life could have been if you decided to pull down your mask and reveal yourself? Who was Mitch deep inside? Would it have mattered if you showed us your truth? Did you plan to end your life all along? If you did, was it because you were afraid to show us the real you? Or were you always being pulled to the other realm? Were the souls on the other side calling you back? If so, why? Did you have a mission we were not privy to, Mitch? Was this all a part of God's grand plan? Did this family need to heal without you? Did each of us individually need you to die to deconstruct our own truths? I wonder.

Since I got home from Japan and New York, I've been struggling with the choice to be a writer, to be a successful business man, to seek the truth through your death, to earn a certain amount of money, to date a certain type of girl, to be courageous, to be happy, to listen to the voice within, to do this and to do that which revolves around a particular construct that my conditioning, my society, and culture have embedded into my experience. As I learn to live with my grief always around the next corner, I fear a crushing blow to the stomach that brings me to my knees. I fear I may end up losing my mind. Right now, I put on my mask because I still choose to fight who I am. Despite my Japanese solitude when I first caught a glimpse of the love within, I still remain blind. I'm medicated. I'm lost. I'm programmed. I'm scared. I lack the drive at times for further self-enquiry.

In essence, I'm loveless. But I know better, even though I'm hiding my inner glow. I feel the healing potential, the desire to connect and build true intimacy with myself. But do I dare to show the world the real me? Or do I wallow in grief and self-pity? I know self-pity was your favorite habit. This is what grief has done to me. Surviving your suicide has left me changed, but whether it's for better or worse has yet to be determined. Will I continue to run from what I reject? Or will I trust and surrender – those words I heard at your grave? What is true? Why do I fight the truth, Mitch? Why is it comfortable in the dark? Can we find the gold in the dark?

If I voiced these questions and concerns to family or friends, they'd think I was crazy. The fear of being an outcast, an oddball, or a lunatic keeps me silent. Sydney is a funny place like that. Everyone is scrambling, climbing, chasing, crawling for everything: the job, the house, the car, the boat, the house up the coast, the this, the that. There is absolutely nothing wrong with having a lot of money, but when I look around and see everyone with their masks on, myself included, living up to what we think we should be doing and feeling, I see self-doubt. When you were on the road to recovery and working with Dad in his office, you were a good worker but you were playing the role of some other guy. It wasn't so much that you were putting up a front to disguise your shadow. We knew all about that side of you. But behind those dimmed eyes, you put up a front because you were afraid of your light. Your light! That brilliant, glowing, truthful, pure genius! That natural flow of spirit that we see in anyone when we feel their love. That exists in all of us, right?

When did we become so unnatural? Why did you commit such an unnatural act of violence on yourself? Why do we persist going against the grain of life? What are we trying to prove? How do we not see our own perfection? Our minds are so powerful with so much capacity to create, and our heart's love is so potent in its ability to help us grow. But here we are, Mitch, living with this disconnected, misguided approach and what the fuck does it all matter anyway because you are gone? You are gone.

Your suicide has lifted the curtain on the falsity of my life. Screw everyone else and their masks right now. I'm talking about family and me. Us. When you dropped that bomb on our lives right smack in the middle of the living room, blowing down the house, you left a giant question mark sitting on top of the rubble. Who do you want us to become now? If we drop the masks and reveal our inner light, is there a chance we can repair the damage to this house? If we fix our house and fill it with new furniture made only with love and paint the walls with wisdom and truth, can we inspire and help others whose houses have collapsed? If the answer is yes, I want to do it. I want to try. I want to know the man behind the mask.

I'm listening,

Marsh

MITCH TEACHES ME TO HANDLE SELF-DOUBT

LIFE BECOMES A prison behind a mask. The essence of who we are grabs the bars of the cell around our spirit and shakes them ferociously. Let me out, let me out, let me out! We try to please other people. We live someone else's life. Unfortunately, it takes a hard hit like loss to bring us to our knees where we're asking life's bigger questions.

Losing a loved one to suicide or tragedy can be the trigger to face the truth of yourself. The question is – are you willing to go there? What are you hiding beneath the surface? What's begging to be let out? What are you afraid of and why? Are you willing to face the truth and discover what's possible for your life?

I knew there was something extraordinary for me to explore after Mitch left us. The temptation, though, was to distract myself. What would I find? Who would I see? Looking within was going to be too painful, I said to myself in the beginning. And so it was. I pretended that none of it was happening and I became angry, cynical, and indulgent.

But when I suppressed my authentic self, I was living in denial of who I was, with all my flaws and insecurities. I became the man with the mask. My mask became my prism and all the qualities that made up the whole of me screamed to be let out, while I remained trapped. The problem is, if we don't investigate our authentic selves, including our shadow, it becomes a force capable of destroying our lives and the lives of our family. Take it from me. What you reject about yourself and what you bury will ultimately use you to your own detriment. It might manifest as addiction, lack of clarity, confused thinking, relationship problems, and lack of self-love. Long story short, you won't be living in the honest rhythm of your own heartbeat.

My suggestion is to use it. Whatever you buried has to come to the surface in order to be released. Once you seek the benefits of the totality of who you really are, you will have endless opportunities for growth. When you reject your reality, your authenticity, your true self will war against you and keep you struggling.

When you really look at grief and challenge, you can begin to see enlightened experiences that will show us who we really are. This kind of discovery teaches you to be more compassionate and forgiving so you can live in perfect balance and order. I have no doubt that Mitch was sent as a guide for me to release my authentic self. It was time for me to stop wasting time, to stop being the false man behind the mask, and start being who I really was as I embraced my the light and my darkness. When you live from your truth, you serve the world. When you show up with love on your chosen path and show the world who you are, it is reflected right back at you. Be fearless, be a creator, and understand that everything that happens to you in your life is an opportunity for growth.

You've suffered, you've grieved, you've been through pain, you've worn the masks. So what are you going to do with all this? What are you getting from remaining stuck in that situation? What are you avoiding? Trust that there is a divine recipe just for you. Use your suffering to take you one step closer to knowing how you can serve this world. When you find your truth, you find your freedom. When you find your freedom, everyone can bask in the GREATNESS that is you.

LETTER 12:
BACK TO THE FUTURE

May, 2007

Dear Mitch,

You know my favorite movie of all time is *Back to the Future.* It's the only movie I can watch over and over and never get bored. I'm obsessed with this construct of time, maybe to my own detriment. I've had panic attacks about being late for the cinema. I get sweaty watching a microwave clock tick down when I reheat pasta. When is the exact right time to pull it out? What if I miss it by a second? I feel my jaw clench at the thought of it and then I think about you. How come we were so late to rescue you?

What would you have done if I had busted through the hotel door at Star City Casino moments before you put yourself to sleep? Would you have been happy to see me? I'd have been pretty happy with my timing on that. Or would I have been an unwelcomed suicide gatecrasher? I may have been the hero of the day, but how long before your calculated mind masterminded a more foolproof plan without your little brother hitting eighty-eight miles per hour in his DeLorean, ready to spoil another attempt at bye-bye? I'm coming to grips with the fact that no matter what anyone of us did, your mind was made up a long, long time ago. Was there a reason you pulled the release chord at twenty-six years old? Was it just your time?

Time. Yes, I'm obsessed! How does the clock play out when you die?

Does the formless world care when you make it to the pearly gates for your appointment with the archangels? Are you busy flying to meet different souls that call your name, who need your help or who want to visit old family members and friends while they sleep at night? Do you sweat the clock like we do here, that your needs won't be met on time? Do you feel stiffness in your shoulders and your throat closing? Do you recall what you did yesterday on your journey and does it matter? Do you cling and attach to yesterday and fall down a well of would haves, should haves, and could haves? Tomorrow, when the sun peaks up from the horizon, do you hope and pray that it delivers something brighter than the day before?

I can feel my jaw clench again. I never used to do that. Now, I'm holding anger in my jaw that won't subside. Suicide can turn a person into a victim when you review relationships you screwed up, poor, lazy life decisions, and personal judgments about delusions. There's frustration in there too. Why can't the answer to death be apparent in one forty-minute meditation? I have a hint of jealousy. I wish this bad dream never happened. Intense bouts of anxiety paralyze me. I grip my desk at a flashback of carrying you on my shoulders out of the church. I need cold water and an oxygen tank, STAT! Rage rises up when I think about what you did. Six makes us family. Five makes us incomplete.

I got this jaw-clenching thing from you. I saw it more and more in your later years. I refer to your later years like you were a fossil when you died. It just seems so long ago that I saw you free from pain. I would watch you closely from the side and see the muscles clench around your bottom jaw. It happened when your mind was ticking overtime, probably replaying an old, meaningless story that had no significance in the present moment. Or when I was driving with you and saw you exhibit an abrupt road-rage outburst that reminded me of scenes from *The Exorcist*. That fierce dude was not the brother I grew up with. I didn't know that other guy who carried the dark clouds of the past and had such a bleak outlook for the future. It was as if love left the building and deprived you of your right mind.

You were a different person in your earlier years. I recall you in your early teens when girls would flock to you at the bus stop, flicking their hair back and laughing while you talked. Everything seemed to be happening in slow motion and I was in such admiration of you. I looked up to you around these girls or on the football field and thought, "Yep, that's my big brother, Mitch." You'd have them all eating out of the palm of your hand. I saw a magic smile with those blonde wavy locks. You appeared to be in your element. There seemed to be a comfort in being you.

It's funny how that eight-year old admiration became detestable when I was in my late teens. That was because of my disappointment in you and myself. I looked up to you, Mitch, and I followed your lead, a dangerous lead for a younger man without the knowledge and experience of wisdom. The foolish decisions you made, the people you hung around with, the abuse you did to your body, your lack of desire to move forward with your life, the way you let it defeat you. When you were stoned or drunk, I saw your resistance to the present moment. What couldn't you bear?

Easy to judge from where I'm standing. Who I am to talk? I have a conniption if I'm half a second late. I'm holding onto the past so tightly, I practically snap a hamstring when I try to run. The mind can act like a magnet sometimes, can't it? I want to break free of the shackles and leap and bound right now, gaining a healthy momentum into the future. I want to feel fluid in my body. Mitch, why do we feed the past when it doesn't exist? Wasted food, no? You were only a few hearty meals away from nourishment if you'd chosen to sit and be present at your own table. The junk that you continually ingested could have been flushed away and restored with one vital ingredient – love. Looking back over our shoulders is nothing but a memory that we can choose to hold in our hearts with fondness, or hold in our heads, missing the beauty of what's in front of us. I know the memory you clung to. It was your test of faith that you weren't willing to endure with an open heart. It was your childhood, Mitch.

There was a time when things were good. We didn't know how good they were, that's how good they were. When I was nine, I had only just begun to take on my own identity. Before that, I remember seeing every-thing and everyone as somehow joined together. There was no separation. I only felt a magical union. The world was somehow all one. And in that oneness there was no time. Everything was just happening. It was perfect. There was no meaning. All I felt was love and I remember how effortless it was. It was natural. I didn't have to do anything or be anyone. I could just be me, a little piece in the grand puzzle of life, driven by a constant, ever expanding, limitless love. It was a type of drunkenness. Drunk in love for everyone and everything. We were at play and life was playing with us. Yes, we were children, but what's the difference? That love never changed. The physical make-up of our bodies didn't change. But how we watered our minds did change.

I had a reverence for my surroundings – the waterfront, sitting on the edge of the jetty with my feet in the water watching the fish. I recall the gentle lapping of the water on my shin that sparkled out to sea for miles and miles, sprinkled with exquisite diamonds. Life was rich and majestic. I loved the lush green grass under my feet that rooted me into the earth. I was steady and connected. I was balanced in the simplicity of each moment. One foot at a time, one thought at a time, one moment at a time, all synchronized in an effortless flow. The beautiful gardens, the flowers and plants that Mum watered with so much love. There were azaleas, roses, cumquats, mango, grapefruit trees, lemon trees, gardenias, camellias, and agapanthus. Our neighbors felt like family. From the eyes of this nine-year old boy, we were all family. It was if they had to be. There was no other alternative. Everything was happening in slow motion. I could feel wonder and delight in the present moment. There was no time to worry about the past or the future. There was too much grace right where we were.

I can see how the sensorial delights that I just described may have been interpreted differently by you. You were more attached to the material pleasures that came with our privileged lifestyle. The Boston Whaler in which you raced around Middle Harbor with your friends, Dad's 40 foot Sea Ray where you lounged, the latest clothes and gadgets, the house in Aspen, and the holidays here and there. I can see now how much you identified with what you had, as opposed to who you were. Mitch was rich and when rich was gone, who was Mitch?

When the banks came and took everything, you were without your physical home. Your real home, your family, never left you, but around this time, we witnessed you leaving us. You separated from us because you separated from yourself. I never felt homeless because we had the strength and love of amazing parents, but you were homeless, weren't you? If we were meant to leave that home and all that we had, did we really belong there? Do we belong in any one place forever? When I think of this, I contemplate death. Nothing we hold dear in our hearts lasts. Nothing.

Everything dies, everything ends, Mitch, and that's just the way life is. You held on tightly to something that disappeared, that no longer existed. Life moved on and you didn't. But if you're not moving with life, what are you doing?

It's no wonder you never returned to your right mind. Your mind became too distant from your heart. Didn't you see that this was a test of faith for everyone? As a family, we were all in this together. But when you chose to let go of the raft and drift away from the people who loved you, what did you have? When you distanced yourself from the people who cared about you the most, how could you feel the love inside you? I think about that and I look even deeper. Come deeper with me, Mitch. If all things, people, places, nature, and everything else come and go, maybe we never really are home in the physical sense. We are in this world for a time, but are we *of* this world? Are we always homeless, Mitch?

We are constantly at home through the lens I described as a child – the unity, the love, the connection with everything and everyone. Is love our home? Maybe it's the one and only home we will ever have. Are you with me? Do you see the paradox and the irony? If we were to know that and walk around like it was true, then we would always have what we want without the separation. Can we have our cake, our heart's desires, and eat it too? Can we live and breathe those dreams? If we can, I'm setting the clock back to November 12th, 1985, and drilling into you what you forgot. What we all forgot.

I now have my own test of faith – a life without you. This new life has opened wounds and presented opportunities for growth and shown me the door to the love I had as a child. I have a choice. Do I allow your suicide to become a part of my identity? Do I let myself drown under that heaviness? Or do I to step into the unknown realm of listening to my heart and healing my wounds? Falling into this unknown space and giving up attachment to what may come, I'll have to attempt to let go of time. There must be a brighter future. Grief whispers to me. "There's a brighter future."

Outatime,

Marsh

REFLECTION:
MITCH PAYS MORGAN A VISIT

A COUPLE OF years after Mitch died, we took a family ski vacation in Aspen, Colorado. We were all hurting and this was a lovely gift from Dad to make sure we stuck together and felt strong. We'd shared many happy childhood memories in Aspen. Dad had built a handful of real estate developments there, so it felt like our home away from home.

One afternoon, after a day on the slopes, Morg decided to take a nap while the rest of us walked into town. He fell asleep. After a short nap in the living room, Morg said he felt someone wiggling his big toe that was hanging off the end of the couch. He kicked his foot out, thinking it was a twitch. A few moments later, he felt the wiggle again. This time it was more forceful. When Morg opened his eyes and looked down at his feet, he saw a shadow of Mitch at the end of the couch. He froze and focused on the figure before him. He couldn't believe his eyes. He said the image was calm and peaceful, emanating an energy of love. After about fifteen seconds, the image disappeared, leaving Morg somewhat freaked out.

If the story had come from anyone else, I might have rolled my eyes. But those two were best friends. Not to mention that Morg is probably the straightest, most conservative person I know. I sometimes ask him to retell the story and when he does, I remember that death is simply a transition, a merging back with the source energy that brought us here. It reminds me that he's home, wherever he is, wherever we are. He's home.

LETTER 13:
LAW AND ORDER

November, 2007

Dear Mitch,

Lately, I lie in bed awake with my eyes fixed on a single point on the ceiling. The point becomes a blur when I lose myself in thought. Is there an order to everything? I imagine years down the road, hoping to know the significance of your death. I want to know who I am and what my life looks like ten, fifteen, twenty years from now. Will the pain of your passing dictate and define the rest of my life? Perhaps if I allow it, that will be my reality. Perhaps if I use it for something else, a new direction or potential, that too will be my reality.

When I blink and refocus my eyes, I can see my spot on the ceiling again. This doesn't mean I'm going to sleep deeply tonight. It means I'm just getting started. The room is always quiet. Everyone goes to bed at the outrageous hour of 9 PM as you know. Early to bed, early to rise. The way it's always been in our house. Now is my time to sit with you. I lost you about ten years ago. There's this itch to reconnect with you, to understand you, to learn from you and to be more than just brothers who had a mutual respect for each other. I want to be best friends.

My bedroom door is closed so no one can hear me speak to you. Do you ever hear me? I believe you do. When I finish talking, I listen. I lie in bed and I do my best to sink into my body. The warmth of the blanket, the duvet, and the support of the mattress make me feel like I'm in the womb and the gentle glow of the bedside lamp allows me to find my spot on the ceiling.

Life without you is here. This is my new life. Things are different. I am different and I listen to you. I wait patiently to hear your voice. Some nights I don't hear a thing, except for a handful of crickets outside. But I see images of you. Headshots. Never full body shots. You're smiling and happy. They flash and then they fade. I can't control what comes up. It just appears. You're a teenager in some flashes and then an adult in others. Although your adult years didn't contain the light of childhood in your eyes, you're still smiling. It's nice to see you happy. Other nights, I hear your voice. I hear one-liners you used to say to me like, "What are you doing, Shonky?" I never knew why you called me that, but it always made me smile. I hear you say, "All is okay. You're okay." I want to believe you and deep, deep down I know it's true, but this is a new bag of chips for all of us. I can't say I love the taste. I loved the old ones, even if they were going stale.

I never hear you apologize for what you did. Some nights I wait and wait for that to come but it never does. Still, I feel your love for us and I guess that's enough for now. But if all I hear from you is that everything is okay and all is fine, does that mean that there's a perfect order to everything? Did you die for a specific reason? Tell me. When I hear you say everything is okay and I see you smiling, maybe that means there's nothing to forgive about your choice to leave us. Maybe we don't need to forgive ourselves for not saving you. If everything is always okay and always will be, are these just misconceptions we've been fed about life and death? Did you really die? Did you go when you were meant to? I ask because I have a story I want to tell you. You know the first part. You started it right before you threw your seat at the table out the window.

This is pretty eerie, buddy. How's this for a mother's intuition? It was a desperate cry for help that could only be heard by a mother's finely tuned ears, that deepest connection at the soul level where there seems to be no time. I can only imagine the scene in your hotel room, those desperate hours. I'm not convinced you knew what you were getting yourself into when you drank and swallowed some pills to put yourself to sleep. You placed a plastic bag over your head. Your eyes blinked for the last couple of times while you faded away and you realized that this was real. This is the choice you made and now there's no going back. Was it really your time? You called Mum's name and she heard you, no matter where you were. Just call her name and she'll be there. You called Mum's name and she would have been there. If only she knew where. If only she knew where, Mitch.

Mum was in the car with Morg, driving to the other side of the city, a trip she made countless times. But this time, as she crossed Sydney Harbor Bridge and entered into the Eastern Distributor Tunnel, she was struck with crazy confusion. There was a fork in the tunnel. She could take the Bondi exit or the Randwick exit, a drive she did thousands of times. They were on their way to Paddington and any Sydneysider would take the Bondi exit.

As the fork got closer, Mum said she became sick and hysterical with confusion. "I don't know where I am! I don't know which way to choose! Morgan, which way?" she yelled.

"Bondi, take Bondi," Morg calmly replied.

Mum took the Bondi exit and looked down at the clock on the dashboard. It was 4 PM. She thought of you and wondered where you were. It was like she was receiving a message from the ethers. That was your cry, wasn't it? Your urgent call for help. You might have done things differently if you knew there was no going back, right? We later found out that 4 PM was your time of death. Did you try to scramble back? Did you slip out of your body and see yourself in the hotel room? What did you think about that? Did you find what you were looking for? Or did you want to back peddle toward new hope? This was the most critical choice of your life, to die on your clock or go on and live. We would have accepted you back with open arms. You know that, right? If you wanted to change, we would have helped facilitate that. But you had to be ready and willing. Were you?

One of the hardest things to digest about your suicide is that you decided to play God. Free will leaves people like you, Mitch, an option to check out under your own supervision. I'm shaking my head right now. Supervision. What kind of super-vision is suicide? There's nothing super about the type of vision you had for your life. Did you have a vision for what might have been? Did you want children and a family of your own?

Did you see your relationship with Matt as renewed and healed? There was that possibility. Matt would have been absolutely open to that. Matt wouldn't have given up. Or was your lack of vision a part of the plan?

What does it feel like in the depths of defeat? Does your vision become a clear path to the heavens? We associate heaven with light, but your pain and defeat were dark. When you can't manage to steer yourself back towards the light on Earth, maybe the only other path is to walk into the light on the other realm. Is there an inner knowing that everything will be okay on the other side? Is that what you knew? Was that your vision?

My vision of the other realm is one of light and warmth. A deep-rooted knowing tells me that heaven is light. That gives me comfort. Are you okay with the other spirits and angels? Did God speak to you? How did you know that dying would be better than living? Did you feel an intuitive faith that you would be free of pain if you chose death? How did you know that pain wouldn't follow you? Were you through learning from your life challenges? We all have them. They're signposts to address a challenge and grow, no? You lost faith in yourself and any vision for what your life might have been, but was your faith in God unshakable? Or was there no faith in anything? Only darkness? Are you okay with what happened in your death? Was anything, even a burning hell, better than what you experienced every day?

Mum pleaded with you to change your attitude and your response was, "I can't." Not "I won't." Not "I'm having trouble." Not "I don't know how." Not "I need help." I can't. I saw this as deceitful and manipulative towards Mum, an attempt to get your own way. You refused to take responsibility for your actions. That's the frustrating part. The "I can't" attitude makes me angry. I'm angry that you didn't want to try. I'm angry that people loved and supported you, but you couldn't see or feel that. Your adamant refusal to accept help makes me angry. Your refusal to want to help yourself makes me angrier. I see why you checked out. What was the point of you being here if this was how you were going to live your life? What happened to the guy who *could* on the rugby field?

You drive me nuts, Mitch. You were surrounded by heaven each and every day. Yes, there were rough and tough days and weeks and months. But there was beauty and it surrounded you. You had a family that loved and needed you. You were a vital piece of our family unit. You drive me fucking crazy! I wonder if there is an order to life? Did you have to go when you did?

You were at a crossroads, weren't you? You were on the fringe. But if "I can't" always prevailed, maybe you had this planned all along. You were waiting for the right time to execute your plan and leave us with the mess to clean up. You shit. How can you be free from your living hell while we're living it? Why are we so upset? When I think about it, it isn't logical. We should be happy that you're gone. If life was that miserable and unbearable and suicide was going to free you of that existence then, Yippie!! You're happy, so doesn't it make sense we should be happy for you? Okay, we don't get to physically see you everyday but knowing you're happy elsewhere roaming free, isn't that enough? Why should we suffer constantly? Why have we been taught that suicide loss is a horrible weight to drag through life? Why have we been taught that grief is a bad thing?

In the early evenings I walk down to Balmoral Beach. I gaze out at the water and I stare up at the clouds. I think about the order to life and see it before my eyes. I see the continuous flow of nature and wonder if I'm going crazy. You've opened my eyes Mitch, but it goes against my mind and what I've been led to believe. You didn't just sucker punch me in the stomach. This was a sucker punch to the soul. Now I look more deeply at things. Clouds do not have a start and end date. They are always in continuation and transition. There can be no clouds without the water and the wind and the sun. There can be no rain without the clouds to feed the ocean. Nothing is ever fixed. One person leaves this planet and another is born. People come and go. I see the transition. I see the flow. But somehow I can't believe that suicide is within the flow of life.

You broke the flow and in turn, you broke us. God gave us freewill. I forgot about that. Maybe there's no law and order to the flow. That's the paradox. Everything that does and doesn't happen is in the flow. It's as unpredictable as the shape and form of each cloud. I guess it doesn't matter. It's still a cloud. And you were you, like all of us, passengers passing through. You were a brother I lived with for twenty years and then you were gone. As you should be, when you did, and how you did. That's it. Perfect timing? Nah. Bad timing? Nah. It just happened. It changed everything, but it happened.

I stare up at the storm clouds brewing out at sea, and I see that more change is on the way. I'm headed back inside to distract myself for the night. Too much of you on my mind combined with this deep thinking, and I'll forget to smile. Maybe this inquiry will produce a smile soon. For tonight, I need a solid belly laugh. Seinfeld will do.

I don't think I'm scared of death.

Marsh

MITCH TEACHES ME ABOUT THE FLOW OF LIFE

AS I CRACKED open and went deeper into self-discovery, more questions came with the territory. I was particularly interested in the balance and order of life, desperate to peer into the future and see the new world that was created as a result of losing Mitch.

Every decision we make opens up a whole new world, especially when it comes to turning points in life. In each new world, there are new people, new interactions and experiences, new lessons, new possibilities, and new potential to act and think with love or fear. The natural flow of life instructs us to move with change. If it were only this easy when we are confronted with loss and challenge. We resist. We want to relive the past and make adjustments. In the case of suicide, the pull of guilt drags us backwards to save the beautiful life we lost. It's a challenge to embrace change and continue to live fully in the present with the hope that everything will work out for the best.

The time we spend in nature is valuable. Whether we're in the bush or at the beach, the ebb and flow, the balance and order, the answers are all around us. It's just that most of the time we separate ourselves from the world we live in. It's too easy to be consumed with our own thoughts instead of becoming aware of the thoughts themselves. Thoughts are thoughts. They are neither good nor bad, but the moment we attach a fearful emotion or experience to them, they become a problem. This kind of separation doesn't allow us to see things differently. Separation is a type of closed one-track mind that limits our ability to self-heal.

The clouds above the ocean are the ocean itself. Water rises from the ocean to produce clouds, which will return to the ocean as rain. The trees in the bush lose their leaves, only to grow new ones when it's time. We're surrounded by the constant flow of change, death, and renewal. I doubt that an acorn worries about growing into an oak tree, or a bud into a flower, or even an embryo into a baby. The natural intelligence that surrounds us takes care of us. The moment we come to realize that and feel it in our hearts, we awaken to the flow of life.

A death, no matter how it comes and how awful it feels in the moment, is going to provide a natural counter-balance. You've heard the saying "things happen for a reason." I wholeheartedly believe that and have witnessed it after the heaviest of losses. It may not reveal itself in the moment, but the love contained in our self-organizing and self-correcting universe allows for constant creativity and potential. This is an invitation to stay open to life and ground yourself in it. Death is simply a part of life and when you reflect on it long enough, it produces a deep gratitude for the life you have.

There is balance and order to life. You just need to learn how to flow and not resist. When you resist, you block the natural order of things. You stay stuck. You stay closed. You stay in the past. You stay in your mind and not your heart. You miss the opportunity available to you. You miss your chance to keep growing and evolving, unified with the world around you.

LETTER 14:

SPARE SEAT AT THE TABLE

September, 2008

Dear Mitch,

To keep the body in action means to keep the pain of you at bay. Mum cleans to keep busy. She cooks. She gardens. She listens to everyone's issues. She rearranges furniture and other household items. Nothing ever seems to be in the right spot. She speaks on the phone to Aunty Robin every morning. She runs to answer the phone when it rings. I watched her do it a few minutes ago. Dad throws himself into work. When he doesn't work, he plays golf. Work then golf, golf then work. He comes home exhausted from either or both and sits in front of the television to zone out.

Morg teaches all day and then immediately hits the gym. Weights, spin, box, television, sleep, wake up, teach. Repeat. Same, same. Matt teaches his kindergarten little ones all day, which I imagine are a handful. He'll have his plate full very soon with his first kid on the way. I don't have a clue what he does in his spare time. Unlike Mum, Dad and Morg who use their body to distract themselves until they are exhausted, Matt has extra time to think. I don't know if that's a good thing. You can see his lack of physical activity in the way his body looks. Shoulders have rounded. Muscles have atrophied. He carries the guilt of you, Mitch. He would never tell us that, but you can see it. You can feel it. But trying to get anything out of Matt is like drawing blood from a stone.

The one time we are all together in the same room is Sunday lunch. Week in, week out, we're there mid-afternoon. In the living room and dining room, there's no golf, no gym, no classroom, no household chores, no TV series to watch. There's us and no one else. I feel the invitation in the air to slice into the distraction. Do we accept the invitation?

I watch Mum on Saturday. There's the giant Persian rug under the dining room table, the marble block that holds the oval shaped glass tabletop. Around the table are six off-white upholstered comfortable chairs. On top of the table is a gorgeous glass vase with blossoming white lilies. Looking inside from the garden, the table looks perfect, like it's out of Vogue Living or one of those home interior magazines. Mum gets off the phone and decides she wants to vacuum the rug. Everything needs to be cleaner than it already is. She vacuums around the chairs. She pulls them back to get to the middle section of the rug around the marble block. There's cat fur in the hard-to-reach spots. Those areas are vacuumed and the chairs are placed in their correct positions. Mum doesn't clean under the rug. No one does.

When I sit at the table for Sunday lunch, I glance down at the rug. I wonder how much dust, cat fur, and fluff is under there. I wonder if you're under the rug, Mitch, because that's where we've swept you. I wait for you to tickle my feet or kick one of our chairs and shake the table, sending the food off our plates and making a clutter with the plates and cutlery. We want to speak about you, Mitch. We try, but not hard enough. In the wise words of Yoda:

Do or do not. There is no try.

I feel the love and effort Mum and Dad put into these lunches. We're all here together, even though we are worlds away in our thoughts. I know I am, and I'm dealing with my regular top-shelf hangover from the previous night's escape of madness. Mum and Dad have Michael Buble on when everyone arrives. I cringe at their taste in music. Their selection of food and drinks on the other hand is outstanding. The cheese and fruit plate is out first. Matt sits and reads the Sunday papers. You can ask him a question but don't expect anything more than a dour grunt in return. He's still a moody bastard. Morg will eat only fruit because cheese may tamper with his chiseled physique. He talks to Dad about the real estate market, home renovations, and that's about it.

I polish off what I can from the plate and hover around Mum in the kitchen. I like to make a nuisance of myself and make sure everything is under control. I stare at whatever delectable dessert Mum has whipped up and attempt to break off a crumb to sample, or stick my finger in the icing. She slaps my hand away and tells me to leave the area. I make sure everyone has a drink: a glass of wine for Matt, Mum, and generally me, water for Morg, and a Bundaberg blood orange soda for Dad.

On the cheese and fruit platter, there's some stinky, tasty blue cheese, a soft camembert, a sharp cheddar, a hundred water crackers, bread sticks, Maggie Beer plum paste, olives, olive tapenade, stuffed ricotta peppers, cold green grapes, watermelon, fresh strawberries, blueberries, and the odd slice of rock melon. People know they better be quick when I'm hovering around this plate. I tend to look like a block of cheese before we actually sit down to eat. In the background, the TV is on mute with the picture on a game of rugby or some other sports event. For the most part, the conversations are family standards: current events, sporting results, social relationships, community gossip, Morg and his renovations, and me sidestepping questions about my personal life. Matt will take aim and provoke me with, "Which pig did you fuck last night?"

When we sit down at the table to eat, the void of grief sets in. There's something about sitting around the table and having to look one another in the eye. The realness of the loss hasn't dissipated. If anything, it has intensified. Time heals some wounds, but not all. And time not addressing you, Mitch, is the biggest and deepest wound. Will we ever fully recover from you? Right now that's hard to fathom.

There's no waiting until everyone has sat down. People begin to pick at their plates as soon as they're on the table. There's a mountain of food, but we all think we might starve. It's like we're kids again, fighting for the last sausage, piece of schnitzel, or extra mashed potatoes. In the rush we forget what we're here for. We forget the deeper meaning of these lunches and time together. They are an opportunity for a moment of silence or prayer. I know it would help in the healing process. It's such a simple act, yet so powerful and significant. I want to eat my food, but I also long for this moment.

Dad is the leader of this family and a great leader he is, the best in fact, but even the best need help sometimes. In the pit of my stomach I hear a voice tell me to take charge of the table and speak. I feel the lump in my throat as the thought of what I want to say bounces between my temples. I stumble, I fumble, I can't. I've taken on your, "I can't," Mitch. I can, but I freeze and then dive into my food like it's my last meal. I want to propose a toast. I want to honor and remember. I want to go around the table and hear memories. I want to start the process. I know it will lighten Dad's heart and shine a light for all of us. This is my daydream, Mitch at every lunch. I'm not brave enough. I want to be brave enough. Instead I'm always hungover. I look down at the rug. I feel toxic.

Conversation slows down. We shovel food into our mouths in an effort to get to dessert. Everyone loves Mum's desserts: the cheesecakes, brownies, flourless chocolate cakes, trifles, mousses, ice cream. The list goes on into infinity. We want to fill up on the goodies to mask our discomfort. Eye contact is brief and limited. When I look into Matt and Dad's eyes, I see a deep hurt. It's probably the mirror of my own eyes. In the silence between mouthfuls I feel the guilt on my shoulders and everyone else's. I feel the shame. I'm angry that all we do here is eat and not talk about it. Mitch, you're scattered around the house in frames and on everyone's desk, but you're fading away from this table. The empty seat at the table is like looking at your tombstone. If we can't fill it with conversation, laughter, and memories of you, we might as well engrave the fucking chair with:

Mitchell William Dunn

24/2/1976 – 1/10/2002.

Son to Kerry and Jill, brother to Matthew, Marshall and Morgan,
and now forgotten family member.

I stare at Mum and Dad when they aren't looking and my heart sinks. I feel the burden of their loss and my shoulders feel even heavier. I want to get drunk. Is this the best we can do to express our grief as a family? Are we willing to admit that we are acting out the stereotype of sweeping suicide under the rug? This table is full of food and so are our stomachs, yet we are all empty inside. The void of your suicide has left us floating in space. I think some days we'd like to find a worm hole in this black void of space and travel light years to a new Earth where you smile at the table with us and tell us you're engaged and have found a life of purpose.

This is our way of dealing with it for now. It's going to take serious time. The challenge is, who makes the first move? I already know the answer. I just have to be ready. I'm not ready and neither is anyone else. The cut is too deep. The reality is too grim. The way you died, Mitch, doesn't allow the food that we eat at this table to nourish us. How we move through this and beyond, time will tell. You died with no appreciation for your own life. Now we have little appreciation for the food we eat in your honor. The beauty that was contained in your life and in this family was not a treasure you held close in the end. How do we grow and heal, Mitch, if the food you left us is spoiled? It makes openhearted communication, non-judgment, and a forgiving heart difficult to explore. You disappeared. I bet each of us have moments where we want to disappear from this mess.

I took a drive with Mum the other day. "How you feeling, Mum?" I asked.

She paused and took a deep breath of relief. "Isn't life better without him around?" she said. She glanced across at me to see my reaction. Before I could open my mouth, she said, "I know. How could a mother say such a thing? I'm a terrible mother for saying that."

But she was right. "No, I get it," I told her. "I feel it too."

"You do?"

"Yeah."

I really did. A weight had been lifted from the family and although a few grey clouds lingered above, the hope for sunshine to break through was there. There was so much worry, angst and frustration during your last few years with us. On the one hand we thought you were getting better. By better, I mean you were gaining the ability to handle a steady job that wasn't behind an inner-city bar, working with people who didn't have your best interests in mind. From all reports, you seemed happy-ish working with Dad in his office. You had a beautiful girlfriend and your own apartment. Progress! I never knew what you wanted in your future, but a brighter future was revealing itself one day at a time. From my vantage point, anyway. I guess you never truly know what's going on in anyone else's heart and mind, no matter how much you think you do. My eyes water, Mitch, when I think of your future, of what could have been. But then it dawns on me – you never really did own your seat at the table. Your seat was like the emotional mood at the table these days – distant.

I ran into an old flame of yours the other day. She told me something very strange that made the hair stand up on the back of my neck. "Mitch used to tell me he didn't see himself living too long," she said.

"What do you mean?" I asked her.

"He said he didn't see himself living beyond his twenties, that he was being called elsewhere."

"Elsewhere?"

She shrugged her shoulders and started to cry. "I thought he was being silly. What sixteen-year-old says things like that?"

A sixteen-year-old like Mitch, that's who. Your seat really never was secure, was it?

This story got me thinking about the past. Like how you came into this world. Mum endured an intense labor and painful childbirth with you. It was a struggle. Do souls come into this world spiritually tortured? If so, what becomes of their new purpose in this lifetime? The relationship between you and Matt appeared to be predetermined. Mum recently told me stories of how Matt attempted to punch her stomach while she was pregnant with you. Not once but several times. How far does your relationship go back with Matt? Why were you paired with each other again? What was left unresolved that needed rectifying this time around? Before you even made it out of the womb he was at war with you. No wonder you didn't want to come out and face him.

It didn't stop there. From day one, he didn't want you here to steal the stage. You were such a gentle, sensitive soul. Matt held the authority but no doubt you were here to learn from each other. His physical strength over you challenged your inner strength. In so many ways, you could see that it was there, but with Matt, you crumbled. You hid and ran from him. If you stood up and worked with him to face your own inner strength, there may have been a lesson for the both of you. Matt would have gained inner strength over his insecurities, while you would have conquered your own inability to face outer challenges. I guess this is why we have people in our lives that push our buttons.

After dessert is finished, I leave the table and flop on the couch. It's partly because I'm overloaded with chicken, lamb, pasta, salad, and dessert. But it's also because I wonder how I'll ever get back on track with my life. *Just get on with it and move on,* I hear the Australian cultural soldier within me. I wish it were that easy. I feel so exposed, so vulnerable, not at all the same person with the same confidence I had as an eighteen-year-old. I know my pain doesn't compare to the pain you lived with Mitch, that you knew you were going to leave us.

I can't remember our last supper as a family with you at the table. It was a long time ago. To my left, I see your photograph shrine on a table. In every picture of you, you are young and healthy and your smile is free. In my sloth-like state on the couch, I have a moment of clarity. What the hell am I doing with my life? My own inner strength lights a match. I promise to always remember your seat at the table for your legacy and your redemption.

Mum's a good cook. Ain't no joke about it. You're missing it, aren't you?

Marsh

MITCH TEACHES ME ABOUT FAMILY MATTERS

YOU LOVE THEM most of the time. Can't stand them some of the time. But in the end, family is family. The empty seat at the table was difficult on so many levels. First, the unit would never be the same. Dynamics had shifted and there was an air of incompleteness.

Secondly, the shame and stigma associated with suicide infiltrated our home and kept family members silent. For a long time, we refused to speak in any great depth about Mitch's life and how it affected each of us. We swept it under the carpet. Mum will try to tell me otherwise and make all kinds of excuses, but it's the truth. No malice towards Mum or anyone else, it's simply the truth. Suicide shattered our family.

Thirdly, it changed us as individuals. The question was, how? Did we grow and learn from the experience? Or were we consumed by it? Did we let it define our lives? I've seen and lived both sides of the coin. Some family members have asked the right questions, processed the information, and grown from Mitch's death. But others most definitely haven't. It's each person's choice, but the ones who haven't, are living in a memory of the past. We have to get real to heal. We have to dig up what's buried down there and it's not always going to be pretty. In fact, it rarely is and that's okay. On the other side of ugly is beautiful when we decide to inquire and learn from such a life changing event.

I believe that there are no accidents. I believe that our birth into our individual families is not random. I think we are born into families we are meant to be with, to help us discover what we're meant to work through in this lifetime. Is it any wonder that family members press our buttons? Coincidence? Hardly. These people are our teachers and in my opinion, we are coupled with the button pushers to help us wake up to parts of us that need healing. In this way, we become more empathetic, compassionate, loving, self-aware, trusting, authentic, confident, and less self-absorbed, jealous, envious, uncooperative, angry, and impatient. The idea is to be able to take a closer look at ourselves and grow. What are these button pushers trying to teach us? Why do we react the way we do? What pain point are they touching? Are we willing to admit this and address it? Are we willing to not take it all so personally?

You might be thinking, "Well, my brother bullies me." But what do we know about hurt people? They hurt others. Put yourself in his or her shoes. Imagine how much he is hurting or what dis-ease she has in her body? Maybe the bully of the family is summoning you to stand up for yourself, believe in yourself. I could go into a billion examples in family relationships, but the point I'm making is that your family is designed to help you grow. The task at hand is to wake up and pay attention to what each one of them has to teach you.

LETTER 15:
MAUI WOWI

October, 2010

Dear Mitch,

Don't believe everything you think.
These are the words coming from Dr. Wayne Dyer's mouth as he stands on stage at The Westin Resort & Spa in Ka'anapali, Maui. I'm here for his *Excuses Begone* retreat. This gift came from a wonderful friend from Kenya, someone I never would've met if you had never died. You never met Zena. She is a very special soul whose generosity never ceases to amaze me. Talk about real friends, the ones you used to spend time with before you lost your way. As an early birthday gift, Zena paid for this entire trip! One minute I was sitting in a lounge room at a friend's place in Los Angeles, hoping to land a couple more meetings for a one-hour drama script I'd written. The next minute, the phone rang. The caller ID said it was from a private number. I rarely answer those calls. I could imagine the call center's customer service rep from India trying to sell me something on behalf of a financial institution I wanted nothing to do with. Either that, or it was a call from home but I'd spoken with Mum and Dad an hour earlier. With my Garfield grunt, I answered. To my surprise it was Zena, or The Oracle as I like to call her.

It's amazing what shows up in your life when you least expect it, or when you need things the most. Sometimes life works in your favor and sometimes it doesn't, but even when it doesn't, life has a funny way of showing you it was all part of the plan. I've learned that there are never permanent gains in life, as is there are no permanent losses. My faith is not one hundred percent yet. The gloom and doom of suicide is hard to shake. It still sticks to me like glue at times. But the more I continue on the path of inner inquiry and the more I listen to and observe the world around me and within me, reassuring insights trickle warm drops of satisfaction into my heart. That's my glimmer of hope for the future.

It seemed like you went into every situation from your late teens onwards with the mindset of permanent loss. Nothing could ever work in your favor. The excuses! Look around you. Nothing is completely stable. That's just how the world is. The universe didn't have it in for you. It didn't deliberately sabotage your intentions to be happy. The opposite of loss is always close by. It's fair to say you were rather pigheaded at times. I'm not confident that a weekend with Wayne Dyer on Maui would have put a smile on your face. A paid-for trip to Maui, does that sound like support from the universe? Or is that considered a loss in your book?

More than ever, I can picture the state of mind people must be feeling to choose suicide – tunnel vision to despair and no way out. It may be impulsive, it may be long thought about and it may be calculated, but one thing is for sure. It's desperate. Whether or not there's any consideration given to those left behind is irrelevant. You are gone and that's that. Life is happening with or without you. The instability and flux of life continues. People come and people go. The simplicity of that makes me question what I've been taught about grief. Death is bad, no matter how it comes. Be scared of death. Run away from death. I might have considered running away from death, but death found me. The worse kind. Suicide. Now what?

There's a knock at the door. I know if I don't answer it, the knocking won't stop. I can feel a pounding headache from being fiercely opposed to change. Do I say thank you for that, Mitch? When I consider the flux of life and nature, I feel like I want to say thank you. I want to shrug my shoulders and say, "Well, that was his choice. He was unhappy for a very long time. What will another ten or twenty years accomplish if he doesn't want to help himself? I'd choose to go, too! If he was willing to go, then why can't I be happy for him? There are billions of people on this Earth and he was one of them. He came, he lived, and he went. He may not have lived the "dream life," but not all lives are long. Some are short. Some are long. Some are tough and some are easy. Some have sharp edges and others are smooth. But they all make up the reality of life. Your life was important, Mitch, no doubt about it. But was it significant only when you were here?

You were deeply significant to us, more than we will ever know. But the flux of life has options. We can flow with it and learn a few things, or sit in the shit you left behind. That's how I honestly feel about suicide. As survivors, we think we have to sit in your self-pity with you. But that's a giant crock of BS! It doesn't mean I hate you. Not at all. I love you. By the time we all move through this, if we ever bloody move through it, I'm sure we'll love you for what we've learned from your death. Now that's a different story. You win because you don't feel badly for leaving us. You're free from your unbearable pain, and we win because we appreciate and love you even more for what you've given us. I think we all just arrived at a place of gratitude.

You swing me around, Mitch. Right round, baby, like a record, baby, round and round. I have compassion for you. The dream is to have you back. I'd like to see you with a wife and kids – those little tackers running around at the beach. I'd like to be able to catch them and pass a football with them. The dream is your good health, a smile, and joyful living in sunny Sydney or on this beach in Maui! But dreams are dreams and without action, they stay just that. We didn't act in time to save you and that's what pulls on our heartstrings. We feel compassion and love one day. Good riddance the next. Somewhere in between is the insight and lessons. Maybe that's the balance with suicide loss.

Suffering is guiding me and I'm learning how to listen. Prior to Zena calling me about the trip, Wayne's books and tapes opened me up like an incision along my own spiritual path. I took long walks from the back of Balmoral Oval and up the steep steps that lead into the bush track to Clifton Gardens en route to Taronga Zoo. Wayne's soothing and inspired voice on my iPod perfectly accompanied the sweeping views of the world's best harbor. Nature and Wayne became my equalizers.

Don't believe everything you think.

His words ring out in front of three hundred people in the conference room. I don't see anyone else. I feel like he's talking directly to me. How much of what you thought did you believe, Mitch? I flash back to the night before we lost you. You sat at North Sydney train station with Morgan. He begged and pleaded with you to come home. He was in tears. He couldn't understand your response to his only question, "Why won't you come home?"

"I don't have a home. I don't have a family. No one loves me."

There's that tunnel vision of despair. Where on Earth did you pick that up from? You don't have a family or a home? No one loves you? Please. This is crazy talk. You were born into a kick-ass, loving family with incredible parents. The best Mum alive. Hello? Man, the power of the mind is real. Those thoughts of yours pack a punch. How long were you feeding your mind those weeds? Imagine if that forcefulness of thought was flipped around to:

"I always have a home. I have a loving family. Everyone loves me."

Now what does your life look like?

Don't believe everything you think, Mitch.

I see color. Your black and white world has sprung to life. You see the greens, the deep blues and reds, the bright oranges and yellows. All you had to do was flick the switch with one self-loving kiss to remind you that you are valuable and loved by many, most of all, by your family. Sadly, there was no kiss to a life of color. The thoughts you fed your mind were kisses of death. You broke down every cell in your body with those thoughts. For so many people who complete suicide, the attachment to those negative thoughts breed like a cancer.

Wayne Dyer is surrounded with a glowing light like the energy emanating from a tree. I've never seen anything like it. His presence and humor captivate this crowd of seekers, even though he's just told us that he's been diagnosed with Chronic Lymphocytic Leukemia. He's a sick man right now, but he's strong. I wish you had that type of strength. In his books, Wayne loves to quote the sages and seers who walked this planet. Throughout this retreat, he references the inspiration for the *Excuses Begone* book as Lao Tzu and the *Tao De Ching*. One particular quote sends a quiver through my body and I think about you:

Every human being's essential nature is perfect and faultless, but after years in the immersion of the world, we easily forget our roots and take on a counterfeit nature.

What you fed your mind (not to mention your body) magnified the counterfeit nature of that perfect and faultless child-like nature. How quickly that exquisite porcelain can slip through your fingers.

Wayne surmises the core teachings of our weekend with him into seven questions:

Is it true?

Where did the excuses come from?

What's the payoff?

What would my life look like if I couldn't use these excuses?

Can I create a rational reason to change?

Can I access universal cooperation to shed old habits?

How do I continuously reinforce this new way of being?

More questions! That's all I've been left with since you passed. Some lead to dead ends and others lead me to Maui. I may not have asked to be in this island paradise for a weekend with one of the world's great spiritual teachers, but I feel like this gift of love and friendship from Zena is part of the gift you left behind. Without your death, I wouldn't have opened up books written by Deepak Chopra, Osho, Wayne Dyer, Marianne Williamson, Ekhart Tolle, Paulo Coelho, Ram Dass, Caroline Myss, and Louise Hay. Each road presents a new world without you in it. I hoped you could have viewed these different worlds without your excuses. I wish I could have squashed your thought that changing was impossible. If you'd looked a little further around the corner, you would have seen smiling faces staring back at you.

Once the day sessions are over, we head down to the beach in front of the hotel. I stand waist deep in tropical water making friends with others from the retreat. We share our stories and discuss the wisdom Wayne is imparting. I meet people who want to lose weight and heal relationships with lovers and family members. I meet others who want to follow the beat of their own hearts, free from internal and external judgment. And there are people like me who want to learn from their suffering after a death. It dawns on me that everything in life is about relationships. Our relationships with food, career, spouses, family, friends, sex and most of all with ourselves. Each of us are on our own healing journeys. I see Wayne walking towards us in his board-shorts, ready to take his daily swim over to Black Rock and back. He's on his own healing journey. He smiles and stands with us for a moment, marveling at the water.

"There's something magical about the water, isn't there?" he says.

He shakes his head in awe. "There's something so healing about the saltwater," he says peacefully, gazing at the ocean as if for the first time. He smiles again and he's off with a gentle stroke towards Black Rock, swimming with ease with the sea turtles. I have great admiration for the man that he is. I felt it all day as he spoke on stage, with his jokes, his depth of thought, his knowledge, his height, his charisma, his willingness to teach, doing what was natural. Now I can see his soulful connection to the sea and I realize that he and I are similar in many ways. It dawns on me that I wanted to do what he's doing. I wanted to teach and share. I wanted to learn from the great spiritual masters that went before and those that are living now. I wanted to strip away what I've been carrying with me all my life that now revolves around losing you, Mitch. I've allowed the grief of your suicide to weigh me down like bricks. I've been losing myself in the quicksand of grief, slowly being suffocated in fear that I know deep down I don't need to carry. Besides, since you're free from your pain, why shouldn't we be happy for you?

I want to share the stage with Wayne and be a voice for the people. I feel this pull towards his work and his dedication to living a creative, inspired life. He is being himself and I want to be more myself. I long to be among people for the interaction, their stories, their smiles and tears, their challenges and triumphs. I want to connect at a soul level and talk about the big questions. The surface layer of chat in Sydney that seems to permeate the city holds no interest for me. I need more. I wanted more and without you leaving Mitch, this thirst might have stayed buried for a long time underneath an ego quickly speeding in the wrong direction.

Wayne understands this veil of illusion. He knows about a unified, universal intelligence that is self-organizing and self-correcting. He is the epitome of love in my eyes anyway, and that love expands when he teaches. He fills our hearts and mind with courage to avoid excuses and challenge ourselves to walk down a different street. He says that each new street brings with it a new world. New opportunities, potential, possibilities, and a web of synchronized relationships are leading us further along our paths to discovery. For me, the new street is life after you, Mitch, with this opportunity from a friendship out of the *New York Film Academy*, spawning from Japan and born from your death. There is a perfect order to this, a whole new world created from a single event that ultimately is working in my favor. When these coincidences (miracles is probably a better word) occur, they strengthen me to let go and trust that the world is working with me.

This type of thinking and lack of control goes against everything I've been taught. I believed I had to chase and climb even if that meant swimming upstream. I thought I had to power ahead and force the issue. Now, here in Maui, I'm not so sure. I'm engulfed in an inner satisfaction that doesn't compare with any other experience in my external reality. For the first time in my adult life, the dots connect. I see a vision for my life that is complete. How or when it will manifest, I'm not sure. But it doesn't matter. It goes beyond a career, family, finances, or friends. It's a recognition of a presence within me that feels alive. I can sense who I am beyond the person that I was. There is a lightness to my body. This feeling is more euphoric than any drug I've ever taken, more blissful than eating truffles and it showers as grace from the Divine. The only question is – how do I bottle this experience and take it back with me to Sydney? How do I lead my life in this manner?

Don't believe everything that you think.
Wow. Wowi. Maui Wowi.

Marsh

MITCH TEACHES ME ABOUT SYNCHRONICITY

LIFE IS THE ultimate mystery. Why do certain things happen in life at particular times? Things simply happen. From the mundane to the miraculous, things are always happening. On miraculous days, I wonder what bigger plan is at play here. Is this flare that I see turning my attention to something important? I say yes. I have to wake up and pay attention.

I'd have been a fool to ignore signs that presented me with an opportunity for creativity and suggest it was only luck. There was nothing lucky about the perfect timing and brilliance that orchestrated an event in ways I couldn't fathom. This was far more exciting than anything I could plan myself. It had nothing to do with luck. Rather, it was the universe conspiring with me towards my destiny, if I could just stay open to play with unknown possibilities. The moment I closed myself off to life's dazzling collaboration and ignored it, an opportunity was missed, potentially gone forever. Since Mitch left, I had become more aware of the power of coincidence. And when Zena rang, the deeper part of me recognized it as a miracle and saw what it meant for my healing.

In a way it was the Law of Attraction in effect. I focused on expanding. My self-inquiry and Wayne Dyer were my daily running mates through the bush that was sending signals into the ether for materialization. What was the bigger plan at play? Looking back now, I see clearly that this was a life opportunity, a door opening, inviting me to be the person the universe intended me to be.

It's difficult to fathom the complex web of interrelatedness between events and relationships. Timing is everything and you might notice in your own life when things are flowing. When there is a fork in the road, synchronistic events happen. The key is to know how to identify them and intuitively take action to follow them.

Meaning is what you make of any experience. I could have easily said, "I better stay in Los Angeles and push for these meetings to happen." But that's a whole bunch of resistance based on fear. If I hadn't gone to Maui, creativity wouldn't have a chance to work its magic. Because I stayed open to life and to the mechanics of a loving, self-organizing universe, Zena's gift was a glimpse behind distraction. It was like playing a game of Snakes and Ladders. Synchronicity is the ladder taking me a few levels closer towards my destiny. Snakes were the fear and resistance of the mind that limited my growth and took me backwards.

When you lose someone to suicide or go through a major life crisis, a whole new world will open up. You'll ask questions you may not have asked yourself before. You'll have difficulty adjusting. You will hurt and wonder if life will ever be the same again. This is all perfectly normal and it's okay. As time passes, I urge you to lean into the bigger questions about your life and the world around you. Lean into the lessons and the silver lining. Be a witness to your process and the new world that is opening to you. Ground yourself in your feelings without ignoring them and move with them. When I do that with an open heart and a willingness to grow, I encounter amazing circumstances, people, places, events and experiences that help me on my journey. I ask myself – why am I here?

I believe it is my natural inheritance to love and to be happy. It's a decision about how I want to respond to life when it kicks me down. Will I answer the call and wake up? Or will I ignore the signs and stay asleep?

CHOOSING TO CARE

June, 2011

Dear Mitch,

I haven't thought about you as much lately. I wonder if that's a result of choosing to care more about my own life. Maui did me a world of good and inspired me to continue on this path of self-discovery. The more I read and the more I meditate, the more I witness an internal shift towards a place of healing and an understanding that there's something special for me to give. Meditation creates a boundless space, a platform to broaden and deepen my awareness. However, a tiny cloud of confusion hangs over me. Is this energized spiritual spark a way to distract me from residual pain I suspect still lingers in my bones. Or is the only confusion that I can be healed?

When I think about your journey, there were chunks of time when things looked like they were changing for you in a positive way. You'd made a conscious effort to shed the nasty habits that were keeping you stagnant and in fear. You were in your first year, doing an Exercise Science degree at the University of Sydney. You had been accepted because of the hard work in your final year at high school. I thought Exercise Science was a great choice for you. It merged your natural love for being active with your curious mind. I could see you working with elite rugby athletes. It would have been a perfect fit for you.

Mum told me that your lecturers were impressed with you and encouraged you to go further into the medical field. You had the mind to do that. I remember you coming home with that spark in your eye I knew as a kid. You had a spring in your step. You were eager to laugh and chat. You were present with us and engaged with your family. Matthew and you weren't on the same page, but that didn't seem to bother you. You had structure in your day. You had a car to get to and from campus. You had your glow back. No more smoking pot all day, every day. Your heart was pumping again. There was self-love and care that expanded and had an impact on all of us. Your room wasn't a dark, messy, stinky bombsite. You opened the blinds and there was natural light flowing in. Your room was tidy. There were books on biology, health, and spirituality. Yes, yes, yes! This was the right direction for you. I could see it!

It was a step towards the light, an adjustment in attitude, a letting go of what didn't serve you including people. Mitch was back and what a guy he was. I loved that guy and so did everyone else. You were the natural essence of yourself, a guy with a bright future and the willingness and strength to make the necessary adjustments. You have to admit, Mitch, that you were singing at this stage, right? Not even you could hide the fact that you were feeling good about life. It was a great opportunity for you to take charge of your life and really care. It wouldn't have bothered me if that care wasn't directed towards us, as long as you cared for yourself. It was most important that you valued the love, gifts, and talents God gave you. You had all the love and all the tools at your disposal.

Then something happened. I don't know what it was, but that bright path turned to dark, triggered by an old story, a dispute, or a wound that wouldn't heal. You were cagey with information. You never wanted to talk about anything. You turned to stone.

"What's wrong, Mitch?" we all asked you. "What happened? Can we help? Let's get you some help. We love you. We can get through this, whatever it is. Let us help you."

I don't want help. I don't need help. I don't need anything.

And here we go again.

Eight or nine months of happiness disappeared in a torrential downpour of sadness. The trigger got squeezed and out blasted a bullet of pain that shot you between the eyes. Man down. And you stayed down. I never saw again that same energy, enthusiasm, and love. You turned it all around. You showed us the will and the strength. You had connected with yourself. You had yourself back and we had you back. How did you go from living a happy, purposeful life to sinking with the Titanic? Is it because you were relying on your own strength to pull you up? Was there resistance in that? Did you need eagle's wings to carry you towards the freedom you must have longed for?

Were you surprised that life was going strangely well for you? Did you think you didn't deserve it? I think I know that feeling. When you're on the cusp of a personal or spiritual breakthrough, a subconscious resistance blocks you. That little voice in your head says, *This won't last. This is just luck.* A lack of faith creeps in. If you've been badly bruised in the past, the greater the lack of faith, because you expect a fall. Am I right? Did you subconsciously expect to fall?

Choosing to live in these higher, more natural states of being is easier said than done. Deepest wounds of the past need to be externalized, processed, and healed in order to move on in a positive direction. The fact that you slid hard, Mitch, tells me that your pain ran deep, far deeper than you cared to acknowledge. But if a deep wound can cause such intense suffering, imagine the breakthrough in its opposite. Imagine how your life can look when you understand that wound. Why it's there. What it means. How to use it for something greater. There has to be that potential.

One can't exist without the other. It goes against the fundamental law of balance. To understand this is one thing, but to know it is another. To know takes time, practice, and experience. You have to have faith. You can absorb the information but it may not sink in until your body and your being become one with your mind. To truly know anything, you need to feel it in your heart and that feeling isn't a pinch or an ache. It's a lightness and a warmth. That's how I know your suicide still resides within me. I have pinches and aches. There are pockets of lightness in my chest and like I said, I'm choosing to care more about myself. In doing so, hopefully I can reach a penetrating realization of my own suffering and what it has to teach me.

When you were here, I saw moments when Matt really cared about you. He wanted to repair the damage of years past. He wanted to care, but you didn't. Let me remind you of a story that paints this picture very clearly. It also reminds me how calculated, cunning and manipulative you could be.

Remember the day you came home hysterical when we were living in McMahon's Point? You were drunk, swigging from a bottle of liquor out of a brown paper bag like a bum. You were gravely paranoid. I heard the commotion from upstairs in my room. I came downstairs and into the kitchen where you sat at the table with Mum. You were curled up into a ball, hugging your knees. You were frightened. "I don't want to be here," you wailed. "I don't want to be here."

I'd never seen you in such a state before. I stood and watched from a distance, thinking, "This must be rock bottom." You wouldn't tell Mum what had happened or what was wrong. You just cried like a baby scared of the dark, alone in his room. You were twenty-two.

Mum called Royal North Shore Hospital's Mental Health Inpatient Unit. They said if you were willing to admit yourself and you wanted to be there, they would accept you. We had seen flashes of up and down behavior before, but not like this. The pain in your face and your sobbing was of a different magnitude altogether.

The next morning you were admitted and you stayed there indefinitely. You had taken the first step. You wanted help. We saw this as a positive sign, considering the circumstances. The details of your conversations with counselors remain a mystery, but one thing was clear. They weren't going to release you until you showed some kind of initiation or the beginnings of reconciliation with Matt. You agreed and off went Matt to the hospital, happy, open-minded, and ready to speak with you. We were all concerned for your wellbeing and most of all, for Matt. He didn't hesitate for a second to go meet with you.

By all accounts, the meeting was a success. Matt came home buoyant and hopeful. He saw progress and he was relieved. Two days later you were released and you came home. Matt was excited, but that excitement swiftly deflated as his attempts at refreshed communication were thrown in the trash. You reverted straight back to your normal behavior. Matt asked you, "What's the matter? I thought we were making progress. I want to make things right between us."

"I said all those things because I had to," you told him. "I wanted to get out of there and they wouldn't let me leave until I made an attempt at reconciliation. I gave them what they wanted."

You were many wonderful and beautiful things, Mitch. You were also cold and could lie to someone's face without batting an eye-lid. Your sham of sincerity really hurt Matt. You guys shared a checkered history, but he was ready to make amends. He chose to care and you ran away like you always did, not willing to confront whatever issues could have gone back farther than this lifetime. How many lifetimes have you and Matt shared with each other? The intensity of emotion between you was palpable. Not only did you reject Matt's offering from the hospital. You also showed you true colors late one night in the kitchen. I don't remember if Mum and Dad were home when I heard a ruckus from the kitchen. I could hear you crying and yelling at Matt. I crept downstairs and sat at the bottom, careful not to be seen. The anger in your voice scared me. To this day, I can still hear it in my head. I thought you were going to kill him.

"What did I do? Whatever it is, I'm sorry. I'm sorry." Matt said.

You said, "I just want to ram a fucking knife through your head."

I didn't see your eyes when you said those words, but I've seen you looking like a psycho when you ran through the tunnel before a big football game. I'd hazard a guess it was the same pair of eyes. It was no wonder that after that night Matt slept with his bedroom door locked. I don't blame him. I would have been terrified. I wouldn't take the chance. You weren't in your right mind and God knows what you were capable of. I'd hate to think that you might possibly go through with such an act like ramming a knife into your brother's head. In the end, though, you were pointing the knife towards yourself. I can see how Matt's lack of awareness would drive you crazy. No one is perfect. Like everyone else on this planet, he's done things he's not proud of but he was prepared to change. He was up to the challenge and you didn't and couldn't accept his apology. You can run, but this isn't over for you two. The lessons haven't been learned, not in this lifetime anyway.

Choosing to care makes all the difference. I don't pretend to know the extent of what you carried with you. With all that's going on in the world, there are days when we all want to run away. Get off the grid. Find our own piece of paradise. The world can be a messed up place if you choose to see it that way. Suicide was your gateway to paradise and out of the mess. That's one of the hardest pills to swallow when you lose someone close to you through suicide. You couldn't convince them of a heaven on Earth. You couldn't hack into their mind and wipe it clean of viruses.

I can see a heaven on Earth that reveals itself even more on the bad days. The calming flow of the ocean, the grainy sand beneath my feet, the laugh of Kookaburras in the gum trees, a mother and child at the playground, drinking a tall glass of water. These are signs of a heaven you see and feel with your heart. This is a connection to heaven. You can be loved and safe here as well, Mitch. But when the heart is broken, it's hard to see. There is no color because there is no love. There is no care. And with that formula, who wants to live?

I hope you found your heaven,

Marsh

MITCH TEACHES ME YOU HAVE TO FEEL TO HEAL

THE ONLY WAY through the pain is to go into it. I learned that but Yikes! Couldn't I just side step that one and hope it secreted through my skin or something? If only, right? The idea of bringing up and confronting your suffering is enough for many of us to turn the other way. To place the pain into a corner at the very back of the closet of the mind and bury it. That sounded like a tremendous plan – one for which the ego would have me doing cart wheels. But the truth was that I could run as far as I wanted, but I couldn't hide. I needed to get brutally honest with myself. I needed to get genuinely real about myself and the decision to feel in order to heal. My life today is evidence of that.

The suffering and past heartache spilled into many areas of my life, even though I was strong-minded. I spoke about Mitch's six to eight months of positive progress before he slid back into the shadows because I believe it paints a significant picture to learn from. Like a lot of people, he never wanted to address what was eating him. I am aware that some people absolutely have a lot deal with. I'm not skimming over the fact that people experience severe and intense pain. But those of us who aren't suicidal still have to cope with the ups and downs of life: liberation from the psyche, healing potential, dissolving of pain, awakening to spirit that lies on the other side of suffering, which are all lights at the end of the tunnel. They are the pot of gold, the freedom elixir that can transform how we feel.

I decided to write this story to let other people know that we can use our struggles, our greatest pain, as catalysts to transform our lives. We can figure out how to see beyond the struggle, to crack open the spirit, to see beyond the veil of illusion, and to liberate ourselves from the confines of conditioning. This is a new conversation you get to have with yourself, a new day to inspire yourself to reconnect to the essence of who you are. Suicide loss or not, fear and suffering are the entry point to evolution and self-discovery. They are our return to love.

The idea that we have to feel to heal means that we have to become familiar with pain as opposed to running away from it. Avoiding suffering and fear keeps us in addictive patterns and negative ego behavior. It is possible to dissolve the fear by getting comfortable with it, by sitting with it and breathing in its entirety. Feeling our feelings and being comfortable with them allows fear to dissolve.

I use the following practice that can help:

I close my eyes and become very still. I lie flat in bed or I sit comfortably in a chair with my back supported. When I think about my pains and fears, I ask myself, "Where do I feel these things in my body? Where is the pain stored?" I describe it. For example, sometimes I feel it in my chest around my heart center. After describing the fear and where it lives, I go to my still place and breathe into that fear for two minutes. I allow whatever images, words, or feelings arise to stay with me and I continue to breathe into them. I let them be. I don't judge my fear with more fear. I just become a witness to the process happening within me.

After a couple of minutes, I do one of two things.

1. I think of someone or something that makes me happy. The important thing is to connect to a feeling of love and lightness. I breathe this feeling of love into the fear in my chest like I explained above. I shower that fear with love and light. I beam it at my fear with so much force, there's no room for the shadow. All I can see is bright, white light and all I can feel is a lightness of spirit. I watch my fears dissolving in the light. I surrender to them and ask my essence to release them and restore me to love.

2. I recite a mantra with the above process. Here is an example:

"Inner guide, I pass over this fear to you. Thank you for giving me courage to recognize this limiting belief. I ask you to restore it back to love. I do not hold any judgment over my fear. I give thanks to what it has to teach me."

As a witness to my own transformation and that of others, the proof is in the pudding. Those who are willing to get real and go into their pain, recognize it, release it and learn from it. They make amazing transformational shifts in their lives. It is my hope that you, too, are courageous enough to get real, be yourself, heal yourself, own all of you and love yourself like your life depends on it.

CHAPTER 17:

LISTEN TO THE VOICE

November, 2012.

Dear Mitch,

Over the past couple of years, there have been moments when I've slid back down the slippery slide of limiting beliefs and addictive patterns of behavior. When you left us, I said that the bathroom had become a torture chamber. I couldn't look myself in the eye. I was overwhelmed and terrified by everything and I became quite the expert in sabotage. I witnessed my eyes becoming more sunken and dull as my natural sparkle was dimmed by identifying with my fears.

Admitting the truth to myself that I was the cause of my own suffering, left me nowhere to hide. I had to digest it emotionally, mentally, psychologically, and spiritually. Without that, there would have been no room for faith. Being brutally honest gave me a clean slate. The truth became my energy generator. I now look at the bathroom mirror not as torture chamber, but as a gauge of my forward progression towards healing. I'm determined to see the light in my eyes once more. The gauge is about a six out of ten. My clarity isn't as sharp as a six and has left me with a distorted vision of my life. The gauge needs to be at a ten for me to truly engage in a life of purpose. I have developed a strong inner urge to understand my suffering because I know there is a greater plan and moving through the sludge is part of it.

I've privately returned to your grave a handful of times. Each time I do, I sit and I listen. I wait for you to arrive. There are two times you consistently come to me when I call on you: on planes and at your grave. You seem to like to dance by my side when I am overseas because it reminds you of all the trips we took together as a family. That's when your soul used to sing, when togetherness hadn't left you.

I can see you in Disneyland in L.A and Disneyworld in Orlando, running from ride to ride, taking me by the hand as each ride produces a bigger smile. I see you in Hawaii playing with a flower lei around your neck in a family photo on the side of a catamaran parked at the shoreline at Waikiki Beach. I see you in Hong Kong, mesmerized by the electronic stores. I see you in Aspen snowboarding down Buttermilk Mountain, searching for any jump to grab some air. I see you on The Great Barrier Reef snorkeling over the coral and fish. And I see you and me together in the pool on Dunk Island where I held onto your shoulders and you took me on submarine rides underwater as we held our breath. I see energy and light. That's all I ever saw with you growing up. That boy was such a far cry from the one I knew in my teens.

I sit and listen and wait for you to arrive. I wait for the mental images to emerge in my mind's eye. Normally, I see your smiling face. Other times it's a projection of another city or landscape, another place where I think I live. It's my life but it's not in Sydney. I used to cast off these images as fantasies and daydreams. I never had any real faith in what they actually might be telling me. On this particular day I waited longer than usual for you to arrive. You never showed up. I wonder if I shifted the energy by asking the heavens for help. I wonder if the feeling of having you around me is doing more harm than good. Feeling your presence might be due to my own low vibrations that are attracting you like a magnet. I can't be sure. But it makes sense. Without the distraction of your presence to fill the space at your grave, my own essence gives rise and it tells me to leave.

I ask, "Where?" I wait for an answer. Los Angeles is what I hear. I don't know how this will happen. I don't know when. All I know is that a part of me feels like a lunatic sitting at your grave talking to the air. Thankfully, my ego is playing small today. The warmth in my chest that gushes through my arms and legs tells me I have a green light. Trust and surrender. The how and the when don't bother me. What intrigues me is the why. Do I have to be away from family to heal all the way? Is love waiting for me in California? What else does suffering have to teach me?

There's something blissful about acknowledging the voice within. There's no interruption or static. It's as clear as a bright blue sky. There's no argument or agitation. There's nothing that makes more sense in the world. It's as if I've known all along. The power is unmistakable and unshakable when I speak the truth. It can break down any wall. It is the "aha" people like to say because they feel free from conditioning or limitations.

That's the feeling I have at your grave. You are right. Everything is okay and will be okay. Joy isn't something we lose and never find again. I see myself in a gigantic supermarket and all the aisles are filled with stories and experiences from the past. They are the background that has made up my biology. I walk down the aisles with my trolley and it's heavy, full of too many stories. I look at all these stories on the shelves and see them for what they are. They are events that happened in a reality that doesn't exist anymore except in my mind. Sure, some of these events have created stronger emotions than others, which make up the story, but what's stopping me from unloading my trolley and placing these stories back on the shelves where they belong? Am I afraid to admit to my own stupidity? Do I want the stories to be real? Do I believe they are true? These events have had their days in the sun. They were part of my journey and that will never change. But to carry them in my trolley that is already full? How can I make room for anything else? Where is the joy? It's gone missing and that's what has to change.

I'm glad I come visit you at the cemetery. It grounds me peacefully in the present. The experience never fails to deliver a pearl or two of wisdom. I recognize the charges of emotion within me and now I seek to face them and learn from them. I don't know precisely how I'm going to do this, or who's going to help me. But if I have decided to have faith in this journey that entails trusting that the right people will show up at the right time. I'm open to doing the work that I wish you'd had the willingness to do. You've made me a student and now the student is ready. Teacher, I'm waiting for you to appear.

"He likes the sound of his own voice" has taken on a whole new meaning.☺

Marsh

MITCH TEACHES ME TO BREAK HABITS OF CONDITIONING

SOME PEOPLE WHO have suffered a great deal of pain have said they woke up in the middle of the night with epiphanies and realizations. That lead to days, weeks, or even months of intense clarity and lightness of spirit. They reported that for the first time, they felt truly alive. The old hindrances were gone and they could see beyond the veil of illusion. They were suddenly at peace with themselves and were able to consciously witness life. They felt awe and there was no rush for tomorrow and no worrying about yesterday. They felt better equipped to handle life's challenges.

These types of transformational shifts, although rare, do occur, but my own experience was different. It was a continuous journey of mini-breakthroughs followed by slips into the old patterns of beliefs and behaviors. I found it extremely challenging to commit to my spirit, to feel free from my environment and conditioning even though I had committed to following the path of the heart. I struggled with who I was and what longed to be heard. Thinking about it now, it seems ludicrous to wonder why anyone wouldn't follow what they deem to be their purpose!

I have heard people say, "Oh, I don't know what I really love. I don't know what my contribution or purpose is." I smiled and thought to myself, "Yeah, you do. You know. It's always been there."

But acknowledging it, listening to it, living it and loving yourself is scary and requires huge change in this modern day life. We were taught that who we are is what we do, what we have, and what people think about us. But that creates separation and leave us in a state of fear. That's when agitation, frustration, confusion, anger, overwhelm, and anxiety reign supreme. We feel unhappy and our lives aren't panning out the way we'd hoped because people aren't living the lives they were meant to live. They're afraid to question what they've been led to believe. They are afraid to do something different from the herd-like consciousness. They are afraid to come home to themselves. But how can you be happy and fulfilled, especially after personal crisis, if you're separated from the love within you?

At thirty years old, I was on the cusp of a major personal and spiritual breakthrough as I faced the difficulty of changing old patterns of thinking. Dr. Joe Dispenza wrote a terrific book called, "Breaking the Habit of Being Yourself: How to Lose Your Mind and Create a New One." In his book he details how to break the habits of the "old self," generally full of limiting patterns of belief and behavior that produce the same old unwanted outcomes in a person's life. It requires practice and repetition until new beliefs and behavior become your natural way of being in the world. Sliding back down the slippery slide when you're healing from major personal challenge is a test. Your allegiance to the old self and stepping into personal freedom free from perpetual fear will be challenged.

If I hadn't lost Mitch, I wouldn't have taken this dramatic life transition for the better. He taught me to question what I wanted out of life and to become self-aware about what fed my spirit. I watched him become a victim to his own limited thinking over and over, and to his addictive behavior and lack of self-love. Even though his case was extreme, it was a jaw-dropping example of how staying stuck in fears drowns your capacity for a fulfilling life.

My breakthrough revolved around truly understanding my thoughts. I became aware of my own thoughts as opposed to attaching to the thoughts themselves. I wasn't a master at this, but my practice became more consistent. I could catch myself before I ran away with old patterns of thinking and instead I simply allowed those negative thoughts to pass through me. But I needed something else. I had to rewire my brain and clear out some of the old stories about Mitch. Once I was clear, I was able to understand my suffering and grow exponentially into the person life intended me to be. It wasn't until I arrived in Los Angeles at the end of 2012, that I found the help I needed.

PART THREE:
DRINKING FROM THE WELL

LETTER 18:

A CALL FROM DANIEL

August, 2014

Dear Mitch,

I wish this road to healing was a passive one. I wish I could hand over the reigns to a physician or healer who could wave a magic wand and erase the offending memories, attitudes, and beliefs. Instead, I'm relying on my own strength when things aren't flowing. I'm calling on the fighter within to extinguish the flames of fear. But I wonder if the fighter within is also a form of resistance. The freedom I ache for, I just can't access alone. No matter how deeply I dig, no matter how strong I am, I wonder if I need a pair of eagle's wings to pick myself up so I can fly free from this fear.

I've landed in Los Angeles, the City of Angels, and I call to you my brother to ask for help. Help me surrender to eagle's wings. Let me know the Truth. I want to rely on the strength of a higher power.

These are the conversations I have most afternoons after work when I ride my beach cruiser along the beachfront that runs from Venice to Santa Monica in the ever-present Californian sunshine. On gorgeous afternoons when I can see all the way out to Malibu, I feel like I'm living between two worlds. I'm not talking about America and Australia. I'm in two worlds of awareness – a seeker of truth and a follower of illusion. I've walked to the well of healing and now I have to drink. Why is that such a challenge?

When I look closely at the word "challenge," I also see the word "change." It's the change that's so hard, isn't it? On paper, healing looks and sounds wonderful and is easily accomplished, like a finish line to a race I trained for. The reality is that change is the most active choice a person can make. I witnessed your choices along your path and I'm not convinced that you were committed to return to the love inside of you after your first two semesters at university.

In a buried, dark corner of your world, was a desperate desire for change. I wish you'd listened to it like you listened to John Fogerty. As for me, on one hand, I want to make the change. But on the other, I prefer to stay attached to my conditioned loyalties. We've all seen and read about high profile investigations on businesses and individuals that span years, until a few vital pieces of evidence crack open the case and reveal the truth. That was the same with my healing. My internal investigation after you left has spanned years but I still haven't uncovered the breakthrough I need.

I want to crack open the stories of your suicide that still impact the imbalance of my mind. I'm searching for a vital piece of evidence, and not always in the right places. I need a breakthrough that I can feel in my physical body. I don't want to be stuck between worlds anymore. It's an unsettling limbo that frustrates my commitment to any one thing. My focus for work sways in the wind because there you are, still bubbling beneath the surface. I feel you in my throat. My own will to change and heal is being challenged and needs to be expressed. Confusion clouds my mind. I heard the call years ago, and the phone hasn't stopped ringing since.

It makes me laugh when an auspicious coincidence shows up. It makes me cry when I fall back to square one. And my inconsistency and lack of congruency as to what I value makes me angry. You know what I value most? The spiritual seeker within me. My inner quest to understand the nature of the mind and the soul. My desire to express my healing and the ability to heal others. That's what I value. It's there and I know that's why the phone hasn't stopped ringing. I don't have a voice messaging system that says, "Sorry, God. I'm not in the right place now, so please leave your Divine message at the beep and I'll do my best to get back to you soon. BEEP."

I hope God will pick up that phone and dial me from His private number. From any number He likes, just as long as I don't have a clue where or when it's coming from. Whatever force, whatever intelligence God uses to bless and create this place, I have to say, is so damn persistent. Just when I think I can close my eyes and forget about what I know to be true – DING! There goes that phone again.

The answer is as clear as the sky above my beach cruiser as I ride home. Please God, call again and I'll listen. I beg you to help me listen, Mitch. I want to feel the peace and flow of the Pacific Ocean alongside me as I head home. I want to feel the stillness of the Santa Monica Mountains in the distance. I need help from Spirit. It's one thing to talk about it and understand it mentally. It's another to have unconditional faith. I hang in limbo between two worlds. Talk of surrender is cheap, but what else holds me back?

Over the past ten years, I've thought endlessly about you, death, and my own purpose, the most curious and creative subjects of all. The internal discussions I have with myself lead to a contemplative day-to-day experience in all that I do. I'm slowly finding a way to get comfortable with death. I'm neither scared nor happy about it. I just feel it behind my eyes. It has its own energy that merges with my external world. The further I reflect, the further I get toward dropping the baggage I've been carrying over your suicide. I have moments when I feel my suffering unwinding all on its own, but only if I acknowledge that it's there. Can we ever make suffering go away permanently? Or is it always there and we have to figure out how to manage and learn from it, how to use it as a sacred tool to a get to a higher planc of awareness?

There goes that phone again. It's a cool morning in January in my new one-bedroom apartment on Hollywood Blvd, five blocks west of Runyon Canyon. There's nothing in the apartment except a bed, a tiny wooden desk, and a dusty chair. On the phone is my friend, Daniel, calling from Rome. We met while I was doing personal training straight out of school and we've been great friends for the past twelve years.

Daniel and I are an unlikely pair on paper. He's from Sydney's west, from an Italian family. He loves soccer, he speaks two languages, and he spends money on clothes and cologne. But paper is paper. I'm drawn to his essence. Like all of us, he has his own story to tell about pain and struggle. His began with shattered professional football dreams that spilled into a downward spiral. But during the past five years, he has turned that struggle into personal transformation, which includes helping others live their most authentic lives.

"How's L.A treating you?" he asks when I pick up the phone.

"It'll be better when I get some furniture."

"Outside of that, is everything else okay?" he persists. Daniel has acute intuition and knows me well enough to recognize when something is up.

"Kinda. I feel pretty good. Still adjusting to L.A, I think."

"What else?"

"It's still there. That bump in the road I can't quite get over."

"Mitch?"

"No matter what I do, it feels like I need something else."

"You already have everything you need. The question is, are you ready to rip right in and do the work?"

Work. I said healing was active, didn't I? Daniel has always been direct. I appreciate that, because directness is a struggle for me. I'll dance around the bush all day, more like pacing around the bush, and eventually get the point when the sun is going down. It's a cluttered and jumbled ensemble of whats, ifs, and buts. I take a look around my empty, uninspiring, and depressing apartment. I want to tell Daniel, "I'll start with you when I get myself better organized."

The truth is, though, that I can't ignore the calls anymore. *When I get organized* doesn't exist. That's answering the call to the noise of my own mind and external influences. In the moment, I feel that working with Daniel and getting brutally honest with myself is the internal organization I need. This call is the "something else" I need to help me drink from the well. This is the answer that is aligned with my mission and purpose beneath the noise of distraction.

"I'm ready," I say.

There's a pause on the other end of the phone. "Get a pen and paper," he finally says. "Write down the questions I'm going to ask you."

For the next five hours, we speak on the phone. This conversation turns out to be the next stage in unearthing my deepest feelings of grief around you. It's the first of many conversations with Daniel that open my mind and heart to the perfect balance that exists in this life. Guilt and shame have been awful burdens to shoulder and carry around in my heart. Amid the struggle, fear, and resistance, I often feel like I miss the opportunity to explore and process the bigger picture. For a long time, my perspective has had no balance. But who can blame me or anyone else in my family? Suicide rips the heart out of a person's chest. I've been led to believe it's the most unnatural death of all, about which society shudders, cowers, and judges. And then, so do I.

My family and I didn't save you. We couldn't. But if your desire was so potent to return to the unseen, a realm where you thought you'd be free from pain and desperation, why should suicide seem so sad? Wouldn't it have been sadder to watch you struggle in a constant battle to stay alive? But I have felt responsible. I never had a greater sense of guilt than after your suicide. I loved you so much, but walking through life with these guilty thoughts has impacted how I act on a daily basis. Choices based on guilt have become patterns and have affected my way of being in the world. It feels like I'm bearing a cross for my own crucifixion, a handicap that limits my ability to find joy. I can't stop wondering, *How did I let it happen? How did I miss the signs?* Or worse: *I knew the signs were there, so why didn't I act more swiftly?* Now I'm angry and I feel guilty that I'm angry. It goes on and on.

I feel like I'm on rewind when Daniel and I talk. I want him to tell me to shut up because I've let it go on for years. Not months, fucking years, which have created all sorts of dis-ease within my life. So I'm glad I've answered Daniel's call as I grab a pen and paper. It would be so easy to get lost in the noise again, but now that I've come this far, I don't want to give up. God hasn't given up on me. He gave me Daniel to act as a guide through my discomfort. He's helping me neutralize the guilt in my heart and mind so I can take my first real sip from the well. This is a springboard to help me swim deeper into self-discovery and reach a higher plane of awareness and understanding. With that comes a greater appreciation for you and my life and everything that I've experienced to date, a statement of my clarity of purpose. Most of all, I have a stronger bond with you, big brother, and I'm accepting my place in the loop of life.

Daniel encourages me to write down and answer the following questions:

1. Mitch has taken his life. When have I been guilty of taking my own life?

Me? Never! I think. There goes that Scorpio defense mechanism. I have to repeat the question to myself over and over as a stream of times and places flow into my conscious mind. I see the finger of blame pointing at me and I make a long list of specific dates and whom I was with and what happened each time I've been guilty of taking my own life in some way. I write down the details, allowing myself to feel each experience without judgment or fear of dropping into the past.

Mitch was one of the first people to introduce me to drugs in my teenage years. I recall coming home from school on afternoons I didn't have sports training and he'd be propped up in my bed with a steaming bong on my side table, watching an afternoon cricket session on our old television from 1989. He had no trouble casually inviting me to partake, but only if I finished my homework first. Such a responsible older brother he was to a fifteen-year-old!

There were times he drove me to a scenic spot by the harbor to smoke before going to the latest space documentary at IMAX. Classic stoner behavior – driving super high to IMAX and then stopping at drive-thru McDonald's on the way home. At the time, I was pretty sure these things weren't in my best interests, but I wanted to do what my big brother was doing.

These early beginnings prompted me into further experimentation and drug abuse as the years progressed. I sporadically drove under the influence, a couple of times narrowly missing random police breath testing units on back streets. Holding onto past relationships caused me to never feel fully grounded in the present. So did staying in dead end, soul-sucking jobs. I was physically alive, but a part of me felt dead, as if I hadn't been born yet. The more I stopped and thought about it, the more my hand moved down the page and kept on writing.

2. What were the benefits each time I took my own life?

The benefits? What benefits? How in God's name did any of that benefit me? I have to stop and take a breath as Daniel reminds me about the balance in any situation. I have to keep the bigger picture in mind. The whole is never one-sided. Where one exists, its opposite is close by. Adopting and understanding this simple principle helps me comprehend Mitch's death and its long-standing impact on me.

My hand is becoming sore and we're only beginning. I recall at least fifty benefits when I "took my own life." I'm not conditioned to think like this. I can feel the brain strain, but the more benefits I write down, the more neutralized the guilt becomes. I feel a lightness in my chest, a gentle tingle on my face as the significance of past events become clear.

The benefits of using drugs with Mitch? We really connected when we were high. These were our brotherly moments outside of being kids in the sandpit. They may not have been the healthiest choices, but they strengthened our bond and we had a mutual respect for each other. We were always equals. Our drug use helped heighten my sensitivity and awareness of the world around me including people, nature, and my relationship to a universal power that is always nudging me beneath the surface. I glimpsed moments of awareness with no thinking, manipulating or interpreting. I felt pure sensations without intrusion of memories, meaning, and conditioning. This allowed me to explore my inner world through meditation, a natural and healthy way of experiencing states of consciousness. Perhaps the largest benefit is that I have become a more empathetic, compassionate human being as I make my work as real and honest as possible. I want to connect with people around the world as I offer hope and inspiration through life's challenges.

The benefit of my "soul-sucking jobs" was the opportunity to work with amazing people, to save money, and to travel and make life-long friends in other countries. These new people have served me in business, creative partnerships, and have added to my personal and spiritual development along my healing path. I've gotten the benefits of knowledge, wisdom and insight into the healing power of grief, love, and truth. As I ponder this complex web of interrelated relationships, I see that each of them has taught me a lesson I needed to learn, opening me to deeper love and gratitude, awakening me to the purpose of what I am here to do.

The benefits of holding onto past relationships includes you. I'm learning to release my attachment to a past that only exists in my mind. This valuable lesson has enabled me to practice mindfulness in the present, or as author, Ekhart Tolle would say, "in the Now." By dropping my attachment to the past, the struggle is melting away. My heart is opening to invite new love into my life and freedom from the pain of the past.

How did feeling dead inside benefit me? It offered me a rebirth as I got in touch with the capacity to feel truly alive and on purpose. It's ironic that death gives life a chance because emptiness means you can fill yourself up with whatever you choose. The void of grief and personal challenge helped me create higher personal values. I had to ask myself:

How do I want to live my life? Whom and how do I want to love? How do I want to lead? What do I want to contribute to the world? How can I help, serve and support?

This explosion of questions contains the aliveness of Spirit for which I long. It's like an internal defibrillator jump-starting new life inside of me. When I ask the right questions, I make room for the light to shine through the darkness. Being in the light is another benefit as I hold a place for transformation by committing to be present.

3. How has Mitch's suicide benefited me?

"Say what? How can I even go there?" I ask Daniel. "What benefit is there in not having my brother physically alive with me?! Oh, man."

This is my first reaction, the same instinctual, defensive response to the rest of the questions. I get very still. I want to allow whatever is true to show up on the page. To my surprise, I start writing down over fifty benefits from Mitch's absence.

I can't lie that this process feels good. There's great relief and fulfillment in spelling it out, like breaking out of a cocoon. It's far too easy to let life be defined by struggle and personal disaster. Like Mitch's suicide. Like how my family members have interacted with each other, with ourselves, and with the world around us. We hold onto the pain because there is a strange comfort in it, whether we overeat, take alcohol or drugs, have promiscuous sex, or stay separated from everyone else. We hold onto the pain because in a perfect world, we wanted a new reality for Mitch. We wanted him to have a life that he could honor, filled with love and promise. We wanted his life to be an exuberant expression of his inner light. We could see it. It was always there. We wished he had chosen love over fear, a perfect world that his mind and heart wanted to see.

But guess what? The world is still perfect without him in it. When he took his life, I was reborn. I began to follow a path that otherwise, I never would have chosen. But I did and I feel on purpose. I have the ability to help others. Mitch helped me open the door to creativity, an artistic side within me that had previously lain dormant. He allowed me to ask bigger questions of the universe, the world around me, and to decide what I believed to be true. He guided me to explore my inner and outer worlds. He led me to Japan where I grieved for him as I started meditating, reading books, and sitting in solitude. A place where I started writing the beginning of this book. I wrote poems, books of them, and I had life visions that have manifested closely to how I pictured them. Grieving Mitch revealed to me what I truly wanted from my life.

We also had a rebirth in our family dynamics. Sunday family lunch has become a priority, a way of remembering how important we are to each other and that family is a safe, supportive space, a place of strength, hope, and vulnerability. During these lunches, we see where other family members are still hurting. It doesn't have to be talked about. We just observe how each of us relates to the rest of us.

For me, the lack of open discussion and leadership around the table bothers me. But that leads me to reflect by myself and to have more meaningful, impactful conversations with Mum, one-on-one, in which she opens up about what it was like to carry Mitch in her womb. She talks about his excruciatingly painful birth, the rocky childhood foundations that were laid between Matthew and him, and how that impacted Mum when it was time for Morgan and me to come along. We tell each other our intimate memories and feelings about Mitch, the beautiful, sensitive boy, as delicate as porcelain, who lost his way in the shadows of his fear and demons. These conversations heighten my understanding of what it must have been like to walk in my brother's shoes.

One of the most beautiful gifts that Mitch gave me was a strengthened bond between old family friends, the kids we grew up with on Shellbank Avenue, special souls with whom we share a long history. We all witnessed the difficulties that life throws you: death, disease, financial loss, sibling rivalry, emotional and mental breakdowns and other personal crises.

We also witnessed the love – the brotherhood, camaraderie, compassion, joyful memories, holidays, intense love, support and community. These friendships would probably still be here, but they deepened with the loss of Mitch. The other morning, when I woke up and consciously took my first breath, I felt grateful that I'd had Mitch as my brother. Without him, I'm not sure when I'd have remembered who I am. I'm not sure if I'd have learned how to communicate or found the courage to stand up for myself, to honor my life, and to unapologetically own my contribution to the world.

Mitch lit a fire within me to know myself, to love myself, and to transform. He was the catalyst for me to re-discover my inner presence that creates, loves, and heals. In essence, he took his life to create space for me to have my own life, and I will always be grateful.

4. Mitch lived his life, too. Who saw him living his life?

It wasn't all dark shadows, was it? We all saw him. I'm writing about the times when people in Mitch's life saw him do the opposite of what he chose to do in the end – LIVE.

He was alive on the rugby field, his playground, which might be the reason people call it "the game played in heaven." It was heaven on earth when Mitch packed down on the side of the scrum wearing number 7 on his back. Watching him play gave Mum and Dad a lot of joy because he was free. And for eighty minutes, they were free from worrying about him.

I'm writing down a list of close friends with whom he traveled through Europe. They have great stories about the chaos and fun they had gallivanting from city to city with Mitch. It was mischievous, memorable, free, and full of laughter, what life is meant to be!

How about our famous ski holidays in Aspen, Colorado? We skied, snowboarded, and ate cheeseburgers at the Sundeck. Mitch picked me up when I fell and he flicked his golden locks back with his fingers over his horrible undercut. But that was the fashion back then. It felt like he and I were an untouchable unit during those holidays. We were really L.I.V.I.N'. I keep writing and writing until the emotional charge of his passing is equal to his living. The more I can feel the life he lived, the more his passing feels balanced and neutralized.

5. If Mitch hadn't taken his life, what would be the drawbacks?

This is THE BIG ONE! I repeat the question slowly to myself five times. Then I take a deep breath and sigh. I have a lot to say, and to my surprise, I write down close to a hundred drawbacks. Sorry, big brother. It's the truth.

First, there would still be a continuous and infectious unrest within the family unit. During the years leading up to Mitch's death, it felt like a dark shadow was hanging over our rooftop. A lot of that was about his relationship with Matt. For close to six years, they wouldn't speak to each other and they were living under the same roof. No birthday or Christmas gifts. Just this yawning divide that impacted everyone in the family. I wouldn't have wanted it to continue that way. For years, Mum and Dad tried to calm the waters and shower love on all of us, but Mitch wouldn't receive it. Love can't be a one-way street.

Second, we would still resent the relationship between Matt and Mitch. The way I see it, Mitch stepped up and sorted us out by leaving. There was love in that. And there was love in the sensitivity and pain he had with Matt. He said goodbye in the physical sense, but he never really left any of us. He just gave us a new opportunity to heal. Some of us have vigorously taken that on, while others aren't quite ready to embrace the significance of his death and how it can heal our hearts and minds.

Dad has always been a stress-head, the most sensitive one in the family. But he is well-masked as are many men of his generation. If you ask me, that masculine mask is a lot of bullshit and ego. But Mum's and Dad's stress levels were off the charts when they were worrying about what to do about Mitch and how to help him at a time when he refused to take responsibility for his actions or seek help. If he were still here, a clear, open channel of communication with Mum and Dad may not have been possible for any of us. I think Dad is more humble these days. He appreciates life a lot more – his family, his new grandchildren, barbecues, and golf. I'm gob-smacked and deeply touched at the same time when I see Dad on all fours, playing with his grandchildren. I wonder to myself with a smile, *Who is this guy?*

Third, I wouldn't have made the same commitment to my spiritual growth. I'd have stayed absorbed in my ego interests and the path I thought I should follow, dictated by everyone else around me. I'd be less introspective, less willing to discover my unique contribution to the world. I wouldn't have gained the courage to address my past wounds. The bag of rocks I carried would have gotten heavier until I was slogging through life unhappy, disappointed, and uninspired.

You know what else?

Here's Number Four: Mitch and I wouldn't have been as close as we are now. I feel like we're finally a team. Better brothers. He has helped me see this life with a new pair of eyes. He's still helping me transform. He's my business partner on this journey and I know he has my back. Faith and trust are all I need since every day, something new is revealed. When Mitch, a child of God like the rest of us, shows me his face, I can hear the voice of God.

6. Has Mitch's death been of equal benefit and service to me, as opposed to a drawback and a disservice?

Yes. That's the Truth. In this moment, I no longer feel any guilt, shame, or anger whatsoever about his suicide. I miss him but I don't need to cry about it. I can utilize missing him as a reminder to honor love. I honor him. I don't carry him. I honor my authenticity and in turn, that honors Mitch's life.

After answering all these questions, it turns out that I'm neither happy nor sad about your suicide, Mitch. It's just something that happened. It's in the past. It is what it is and your legacy will live on through me. We all had to be born again – as a family, as individuals, as friends, and as "men for others." I always loved St. Aloysius College, where we were taught to be "men for others." Your death called me back inside to remember something and someone I lost and desperately needed to find again. And that is exactly what I'm doing.

Marsh

MITCH TEACHES ME THE POWER OF FORGIVENESS

THE PROCESS WITH Daniel was just what the doctor ordered and he arrived at precisely the right time. One the biggest lessons I learned as a result of the process was the power of forgiveness. The process itself that I went through with Daniel didn't really focus on forgiveness. But the feelings of love and gratitude that I experienced allowed me to let myself off the hook. Here is a beautiful line I heard once from spiritual teacher, Iyanla Vanzant, about forgiveness:

"You must for-give in order to for-get the love that you're looking for."

I thought that was absolutely beautiful and hit the nail on the head. For so long, I didn't realize that I hadn't forgiven myself about Mitch. As a result of the work, I allowed myself to forgive all the stories, people, experiences, and fears from the past. That was the magic. The mere act of forgiving myself and other people for perceived wrongdoings they caused in my life, was a huge weight on my chest and shoulders. When I let go, I felt free. The release was ecstatic, better than any artificial ecstasy I ever took, and without the come down. It was the opposite. It was a "come up." The high was smooth, consistent, clear, and ever expanding. Forgiveness allowed me to breathe deeply and when I exhaled, inner peace replaced chaos.

Forgiveness isn't always easy. It can be a process that takes time, but the time it takes is worth it because with the release of fear is a return to love. How we perceive these painful circumstances in our lives drives how it affects us. We can stay anchored to fear of the past, or we can awaken to a new day – a new day to start again with a choice to be free.

In order to harness the power of forgiveness, apply the following steps in your own life:

Release judgment: Judgment creates suffering at some level because you're fighting with what's happening in the present moment. The more emotionally honest I am about my reactions to people or circumstances, the more I discover what these people or circumstances have to teach me.

Identify the triggers: When someone makes a remark or you're offended by other circumstance, notice the hurt, sadness, or emotion that rises to the surface. Why am I reacting this way? What is it inside me that needs to be addressed?

Own your traits and behaviors: In most cases when we judge what we resent in others, we find those traits within ourselves. I loathed Mitch's self-pity and apathetic approach to life when he was depressed. Those were the same qualities that existed within me at times in my life. When do you behave in a manner that you find offensive?

Be kind instead of right: I like the Chinese proverb: "If you are going to pursue revenge, you better dig two graves." Resentment is debilitating. Choose the high road and refrain from being sucked into the agenda of the ego.

Practice sending love: None of us are perfect. People trip and make mistakes. Everyone has a journey and has to deal with his or her struggles. If you can practice a mindset of compassion and empathy, you can build self-awareness and limit the emotional impact people's words and behaviors have on you.

OPEN HEART, NEW LOVE

November, 2014

Dear Mitch,

Did you believe in miracles? Can you imagine being in a place where you've completely let go of the past? What does that look like for you? Paint me a picture of a world created by a shift in thinking. How open is your heart? Can you give and receive love now without interruption? How does that feel? Your psychological, spiritually unsound way of being has melted away. You're free. Your smile from old family portraits is back. You're here with us now and your heart is open. There is nothing to fear. There are no problems. You made room for new love. You made room for a miracle. Paint me a picture because I want to paint you one.

I rarely use the term "miracle." I used to roll my eyes when priests at school made reference to Jesus walking on water or ascending into heaven, body and soul. Once in a blue moon, I'd sit up and take notice when I read a story that could only be described as divine intervention. I love a story by Anita Moorjani, author of *Dying to Be Me*. It's her tale of healing from cancer, a miracle because of the scientific and spiritual phenomenon that occurred. On her deathbed, with hours to live and tumors the size of lemons littered throughout her body, she slipped into a coma and visited the other realm. There, as she embraced knowledge, wisdom, truth, and unconditional love, there was shift in her beliefs. As her thinking changed, so did her life. Two weeks after she woke up, she was completely cancer free with a miraculous story to tell. To this day, her doctors can't explain what happened, although Anita surely can.

My conversation with Daniel and the work we did together felt like a shift, a small miracle. It opened my heart so I could see you and me for truly who we are. I'm still tentative when I say the word "miracle" out loud because it goes against my conditioning. But a window has opened and I have to acknowledge the miracles that surround me. I'm talking about the first heartbeat of a newly born child, our perfect biological make-up, how fruit spawns from a seed, and billions and billions of snowflakes have six sides like a human finger print and no two are exactly the same. I've taken these miracles for granted but my conversation with Daniel brought up the miracle of our holy relationship. I feel like I'm facing you now, heart to heart. I see you as a teacher who is showing me my limits in my capacity to love. I feel as though we're healing each other of self-loathing. I can finally see you for who you are, leaving all grievances aside. I feel forgiveness in my heart, which says that only love is real.

When I think deeply about forgiveness, maybe there's nothing to forgive. Forgiveness is love. Love is perfect and whole. Whatever fear I've held in my heart about you and toward myself has brought me to this moment of gratitude. What is there to forgive? You physically died in 2002. But these days, in 2014, you feel more real to me than before.

A few weeks after my conversation with Daniel, the world around me feels new, like I have a new pair of eyes. There's a shine and clarity wherever I place my attention. I take time looking at each object without interruption or intrusion. It feels like I'm high, nature's high, the way being high was intended. It sure beats our smoking adventures to IMAX. I'm reminded by my ego with its dogged resistance that this feeling won't last forever. But these moments offer me a glimpse of a miraculous shift in perception that makes me want to explore further. Who am I? Who am I? Who am I? I can read the invitation now and I'd like to RSVP. Whether it's a suicide loss or other life trauma, I see what you have given me. I hope other people see their invitations, too. I want my healing to give others permission to heal themselves.

I have to smile at a breakthrough like this. Relationships are assignments, aren't they? The holiness and depth of our relationship, one that has reached new dimensions in death, is designed for maximum growth, isn't it? For you and for me. Is your new assignment to use me as an instrument? Are you shining your light through me? You may not have been able to save your own life, but is your redemption your capacity to save others through me? I never thought I'd have a business partner like this, but that's how it feels. My healing is your healing and together, who knows? Maybe we can help someone else.

As I write these words I feel like I'm wrapped in the arms of God. There's a warm presence in my body, an inner stillness and calm. I don't have to be anywhere except right here. My heart is open to receive whatever it needs and the love I want to give, I'm putting on the page. It's all because of you. This might be the most authentic relationship I have with anyone, a mindful collaboration of honesty and forgiveness. I've seen and processed my own ugliness and fear as I move forward into unchartered territories of spiritual discovery. However much it stings, it beats the hell out of walking through life unconscious and lost in denial of the Truth. The trauma of a suicide loss has left me with a fractured sense of self and the imposter within, the ego, loves to shame me. It sings in crisis and feeds a song of misery as I vibrate in grief and fear. It's a brighter day when I can see things differently, when I say out loud, *I am willing to see things differently.* It's all because of you. You are my miracle.

I've been blessed with another miracle these days, a beautiful woman named Amanda who has come into my life in the midst of transition. Like you, she is helping me grow into the man I want to be. Amanda's name means "worthy of love," and through her, I have the opportunity to explore places within that have yet to be discovered. It's rigorous work but our honest dedication to each other brings out our capacity to transcend our own lives. You know these people when they show up in life. You can't miss them. She's the lady in red in a room devoid of color. We're pushing each other's buttons to awaken what needs healing and the timing is a mysterious, wonderful thing.

I believe that everything we need is given to us at precisely the right time. I never had faith in that, especially right after your death. When we experience suicide loss, faith in oneself and the world tends to crumble. But when we are spiritually connected and sound, we become stronger and new light and love emerge from the darkness. We just have to look in the right places, which starts with a shift in thinking. I know that a shift in thinking is a miracle because I've seen it with my own eyes. It has awakened me to the healing power of Grief, Love and Truth.

In grief, there is relief. Through the tears will be laughter and through the heartache will come breakthroughs. Death gives life a chance. In love, fear only exists in the mind where stories are played out. Love is light and a shift in thinking can cause it to shine. We discover our freedom in the power of truth, which you gave me when you died. It took me over ten years to know this in my heart, to hold it in my hands, and to embrace it like my life depends on it.

Amanda hasn't been the only miracle to show up in my life lately. New people, places, experiences, and events have appeared. I told you I never used the word miracle much before, but here I am, at the Saban Theatre on Wilshire Blvd in Beverly Hills on a Monday night, listening to Marianne Williamson's lecture on *A Course in Miracles*. I had never heard of *The Course* until I was in Wholefoods making a salad in the self-service bar when I overheard a chat between two people about relationships and this woman, Marianne Williamson. It was a Monday afternoon and by chance, she was speaking that evening, five minutes from my apartment. Of course, the first lecture I attend is on relationships.

My brother, my brother. You bring me gifts exactly when I need them. I feel your support more and more every day, and all it took for this shift was to show you my wounds. I've been letting down my mask and I feel you laughing with me. It's funny, right? In order to stamp out the darkness, all we have to do is turn on the light. In order to rid ourselves of fear, all we have to do is turn it over to love.

Simple? Yes! Easy? Not quite. We hold on until our hands are sweaty and we lose our grip for fear of what will happen when we let go of our wretched anxiety. If only we knew the comforting hands that are ready to catch us when we decide to let go. Remember my dream? I have no doubt that the deep blue ocean you dropped into from a thousand feet in the air was the comforting hand of God, cradling you to merge back with source energy.

I hope the rest of the family will wake up to the healing power of your death. It has affected each one of us differently because we all related to you in different and unique ways. Each of us has our own lessons if we are willing. Mum has something to learn. Dad has something to learn. Matt has something to learn and Morgan has something to learn. Do they want to do the work? I can't answer that. I have no idea how deep they're willing to go into their subconscious beliefs. Are they willing to see their own fears and breathe them to the surface to make way for healing? Most people find it easiest to walk around in life with a dull ache beneath the surface.

I see that with my family, but it's not my job to change anyone else. That's up to each individual. I can hear Morg calling me a preacher. I can see Dad's uncomfortable silence, not sure what to say, doing anything in his power to leave the room and get to the golf course as quickly as possible. I can see Matt shutting down the conversation and looking at me like I have two heads, his defense mechanism to keep his guilt at arm's distance. Mum is the only one who has really gone into her pain. I don't pretend to I know how it feels to lose a child to suicide, but the strength and the compassion Mum has shown for herself is inspiring. I look forward to having conversations about you with Mum in more depth and detail when I return to Sydney. I have a feeling that a new kind of open-hearted Sunday lunch is possible.

Love from Lalaland,

Marsh

MITCH TEACHES ME ABOUT RELATIONSHIPS

RELATIONSHIPS ARE THE foundation of life, essential for human beings to flourish. We have a relationship with everything, a sure sign that everything is connected. From our brothers and sisters to food, family, money, career, spirituality, mental and physical health, nature, animals, and sex. By far, the most important relationship is the one we have with ourselves. A strong, intimate relationship with ourselves translates into a healthy relationship with God or a Higher Power.

No matter your purpose in this life, it helps to put a strong emphasis on creating and sustaining relationships. It's the secret to improving our lives emotionally, mentally, spiritually, and physically. The more you put in, the more you get out. Feeding joy to yourself and your spirit are paramount. The old adage is true that when you smile, the world smiles with you. That starts with a healthy relationship to your essence and being grateful for the life you've been gifted.

People who decide to leave us on their own terms like Mitch did, have lost the spice of life. As he drifted further away from himself, so did the people around him. Even family members were shut out. If you're wondering why you can't get out of your funk and fears, take a look at your relationships. Examine how you relate to the planet, to other people, and most of all, to yourself. I've experienced some dark times as a result of choosing not to care about my relationship with myself. Thankfully, I now know what makes all the difference. It's love.

If you believe that love has left the building, you are in a fantasy. You were born from love, brought into this world from love, and love sustains you in your physical body. Does your body ever refuse to pump blood because it is lost in fear? The flow with which our bodies operate, the perfect pharmacy that they are, their immaculate genius to supply whatever the body needs, can only be surmised as love for life and creation.

Relationships encourage our natural abilities and curiosity. They nurture our growth. When you find someone or something you love, cherish it, build on it, explore it, and give a million thanks because one day, like everything else, it will be gone. Death will be here and it will be time to say goodbye to the wonderland of life.

Seek the pearl in the oyster with relationships that don't serve you. What is the lesson? What is the relationship teaching me or waking me up to? How can I grow and become a better person as a result of my relationship to x,y,z? Begin to play with life and ground yourself in it. You are infinitely connected to everything around you. Deepen your relationship to life. When the waves of challenge come sweeping through, you'll be better equipped to ride them and not feel like you've been knocked down, chewed up, and spat out.

LETTER 20:

HANDING OVER TO SPIRIT

December, 2014

Dear Mitch,

You were familiar with the word "addiction." I'm not singling you out. It's fair to say that every Tom, Dick and Harry in the world encounters addiction of some kind. But with the spiritual detoxification and healing that's working through me, I have the natural urge to give up alcohol. Crisp, cold beer on sunny afternoons by the beach, delicious negronis before a nice dinner with friends, a Hendrick's gin and tonic with cucumber, and a glass of Pinot or Shiraz with a wintery, hearty meal. I do love a drink, but controlling my intake is the challenge. Like you, I have a hard time limiting myself to one or two in a social environment. I haven't mastered the balance yet and I wonder if that's something worth considering about this. As I've overcome fears in my life, the voice inside says its time to explore a life without the mask of alcohol. Do we ever conquer our addictions, or do we just outgrow them?

To conquer suggests a fight. There is resistance in that. I've learned that where there is a fight and resistance, it's a losing battle because there's no room for love and compassion for myself. When I fought guilt and shame over your suicide, when I directed the anger towards you and myself, that's when the avalanche of fear came rumbling down the hill. It's easy to become buried under the fear, a dangerous predicament if you want to stay in your cave of shadow. You may be able to live there for a period of time, but to be surrounded in that intoxication leaves you with a crippling disability. You can't walk forward because you are perennially lost in the past.

As I write these words, I know I must let you go completely. Your suicide has become my addiction. Learning and growing from it has been my gift. Only now, as I break through and find insights, do I realize the importance of finishing what I started in order to put you to bed. I feel that you cannot fully rest while I'm calling your name. Am I validating myself through you? Why do I have to learn to be a better person through your shit storm? I have to acknowledge that I cannot conquer my addictions. I must learn to outgrow them. How do I do that?

I asked for help recently, but not from a doctor or a religious leader. I knew I had to stop relying on my own strength, which was never enough and left me in a state of fear, a million miles from freedom. When I pushed, pulled, chased, and climbed, I could feel my lack of faith and support in universal power, source, spirit, whatever you choose to call it. I thought I would never arrive at a state of freedom that included focus and discipline concerning addictions to alcohol, food, sex and any other fears. I wanted to honor my life. I wanted out of the constant battle of letting go of you. So I stopped fighting and instead of engaging in the tug-of-war, I slowed down and handed over the process to my ally who has helped me before. I went inside to the power of love that creates and heals. When you have the blinkers on, it's hard to remember that faith and surrender need to be practiced daily. By surrendering to the power of love, my fears began to wash away. That was a miracle.

The liberating effects of sobriety mixed with meditation and prayer have ultimately produced clarity of mind and dedication to healing my self-doubt. My release of judgment combined with forgiveness created a space for love to have the final say. I transformed because I said YES to the Presence within me. When my confidence unlocked the shackles and opened the prison door I was blown away, not so much by abstinence. Rather, I was amazed at the power of prayer and meditation. These two practices and treasures that we so rarely use are available. Speaking and listening to a Higher Power connected me to the breath of life I so sorely needed to create change.

Change is an undeniable truth of the universe, a true miracle. It has been a miracle to know that when my thoughts are free from fear, when they operate from a place of love and gratitude, I can influence my reality. I laugh at the so called coincidences that show up in my life because I know better, now that I have handed my life over to spirit.

For me, the act of prayer doesn't have to be tied to Jesus, Allah, or Buddha. It's not about asking a universal source energy to dispense my wishes. It is purely an act of gratitude and thanks. It is a present moment of centeredness where I feel aligned with that source energy that is a part of me. In the act of giving thanks for my life as it is right now, even with the struggles and challenges, a revived energy flows through me that springs me into action. A restored trust in myself occurs because I know I have help and I can collaborate and work with the same energy that gives life to this universe. I am a part of that. There is no separation. After I have expressed my gratitude for my life, all I ask for is guidance, strength, wisdom, compassion, creativity, focus, and signs to keep me moving along my path, growing more and more into the person I want to be. Prayer is a priority, my daily opportunity to make conscious contact and speak to the universal source of energy and love.

The same goes for meditation where my awareness deepens and becomes super-charged. It's like a warm hug from source energy. I can feel it in the stillness of heightened awareness. Apart from the deluge of chatter in the mind, there is an invitation to expand. I can see heart and soul-centered images and words. I can hear sounds. The perfect movie of my deepest intentions and desires play organically in my mind. Each meditation session is different and I never know what's going to happen, but powerful and creative visualizations, fascinating, treasured experiences, spring from my essence. In those moments, I have the opportunity to see my life for what it is – my soul's journey through the blessing of a physical body. This body gives my soul the opportunity to raise its vibration through its own Divine Purpose.

All the bumps and hurdles that are thrown at me matter. They are there to be loved and appreciated. Meditation helps me wake up to that. It feeds me energy and fuels what I already have. It instills unconditional love and support. In my meditative state, I am protected. I am wearing my spiritual armor. No fears can penetrate because there is no room for them in a force field of love.

When my eyes open, the challenge is to remind myself of the Truth in the midst of a barrage of activity and distractions. If I remember that I am Source, if I let it work through me and feed my mind, then I am onto a good day. If I take that presence and love out into the world and do my best to live it moment to moment, interaction to interaction, I'm going to have a good day. Life flows naturally and the memory of you is just that – a memory. No attachments, no worries, no anything. It just is. It feels so strange to say that after all we've been through, but that's how it feels. I'm letting you go so you can rest while I live out my time in this physical body.

Thank you, my brother. Thank you.

Marsh

MITCH TEACHES ME TO DEEPEN MY AWARENESS

IF I DIDN'T meditate and pray, I'd be lost in the noise of the world around me, and my internal world of self-limiting thoughts. Meditation plugs me into life. It allows me to become completely engaged with life, but not overwhelmed by it. Tim Brown, a great meditation teacher in Sydney, says that we're exposed to more stimulation in one day than our ancestors had during their entire lifetimes. Imagine what this stimulation does to the human nervous system. It robs us of ourselves, our friends, and our families. When you've gone through trauma or struggle, the beautiful practice of meditation is the most valuable tool in your arsenal to help you cope.

Meditation has helped me become a better person. By tuning into my spirit and creating enough inner spaciousness to let it expand, I've become more open with my friends. Conversations that we might never have had, have appeared as a result of opening up and becoming more self-aware. I have no hesitation in asking my loved ones what's bothering them and getting to the root of their concerns. For the most part, they appreciate that as we deepen our relationship. As a conditioned Australian male, I used to shut my mouth and wait until I was drunk before I could really talk with people. But now meditation has strengthened my emotional muscles, allowing me to unapologetically have meaningful conversations about life, challenges, and what's really going on, without feeling awkward. Some of my friends are quick to shut down this type of conversation, but new ideas and possibilities are planted. Perhaps sometime down the line, they'll give their emotional intelligence the space to breathe. If Mitch hadn't passed, I don't think I'd have had this opportunity in my life right now. Today I know that there will always be a rainbow in the cloud. It's a matter of opening up to see it. That's where meditation comes in.

Meditation can help you see the silver living in suffering because the practice grounds you into life. You come to realize that the real you is not limited to your physical body. Until you are committed to looking inside and connecting with your essence, your ego will pass off your deepest feelings as BS. But I can promise you from experience that BS will ultimately turn into Holy Shit because you'll come to know the Truth, that there's a part of you that never dies. That is how I find comfort when I think about my brother.

Over the years, life has given me examples of the continuation and transition of spirit. The morgue, dreams, visitations, coincidence, synchronicity. I didn't have to look very far. The conditioned mind likes to pass that off as ludicrous, but meditation and prayer have allowed me to move beyond the ego mind. I have been able to move deeper into my own awareness to allow me to live a fuller life, no matter what hurdles come my way. I take comfort in knowing that death is simply a part of life. I'm not afraid of it any longer and in truth, no one needs to be. What I fear is ignoring what is inside my heart. It is a waste to carry around a bag full of regrets. Why not lean into the deeper parts of yourself that yearn to be heard? They are there. Don't die with the music in your heart. Sing it loud and be free to be you and only you.

Some people are turned off by the word "prayer." I get it. I've felt like that in the past. But today, I have fun with prayer because I don't associate it with anything remotely religious. Even though I recite a prayer from St. Francis of Assasi each morning, I see this man as an evolved, awakened individual, not just a man of the cloth devoted to Christ. I find time for prayer throughout my day and all it centers on two words:

THANK YOU

I could be having a swim in the ocean, admiring a city view, laughing with a friend, engaged in a work meeting, or seeing an old family photo with Mitch. Whatever it is, a silent "thank you" is my prayer, which I practice all throughout my day. It's a small thing that makes a big difference, especially when I'm finding it difficult to appreciate anything because of the pain in loss.

STARS ALIGNING

February, 2015

Dear Mitch,

Let me tell you a story. In fact, let me tell you a couple of stories. Handing over to spirit, which means believing my own Truth, is like seeing a door to my real life, the life I was meant to live. When I decided to walk the path of the heart, when I began to trust myself, new beginnings occurred. A shift in consciousness produced a re-birth within me and opened the door to miracles. I can't believe I'm using that word, miracle, but that's the only way to describe it.

I've been working at a small hospitality company in West Hollywood. I go there every morning from my apartment on Hollywood Blvd, walking along bustling Sunset Blvd to Holloway Drive, then down Hancock Ave to Santa Monica Blvd. During the walk, I reflect on where I am in my life and I give thanks. The traffic doesn't bother me for the most part, unless a Harley Davidson hugs the sidewalk and revs its engine in my left ear.

A few days ago, I was walking to work like I normally do, feeling more buoyant than usual and reflecting on my intention to live my own Truth. Was I completely doing that? What did I need to do next? What else did I need to learn? What did I want to share? Did I have clarity about my unique contribution? How did I want to live? How did I want to love? How did I want to lead? Why was I being called? I thought about all the time I'd lost over your suicide and all that I had gained since then. This walk to work opened another door in the room of Truth.

I need to finish this book, I thought. I need this for myself and maybe, just maybe, it can help someone else. Am I a teacher? I felt calm and still. Anita Moorjani's book, *Dying to be me,* popped into my head. I loved her story and message from the afterlife. I had seen her speak in Sydney with Wayne Dyer, years earlier. I think it was one of the first talks she gave when her story hit me in the chest. An image of her book pinged between my eyes. I smiled and decided to say a prayer to the energy that produced these thoughts. I said, "Thank you for this sunny SoCal morning and these questions in my mind. I have another question and I hope you can give me a sign. Am I a voice for the people?"

I walked into the office, sat at my desk, and turned on my computer. I looked at my reservations for the day and the first name to appear on that list was Anita Moorjani. Her name was literally staring me in the face. Are you kidding me? I nearly fell off my chair. I laughed out loud and said, "Thank you!" What were the chances? Her email address was attached to the inquiry so I sent her a message. I told her how thankful I was for her story and how completely blown away I was at the interconnectedness of life. That was my sign – one amongst many others that revealed themselves precisely at the right time, all because I surrendered to spirit.

It also showed me that I didn't always need signs. Anita's name was a blessing, but it taught me to deepen my trust. If I feel like I'm walking toward my Truth, why do I need signs? I don't. Signs show up to reaffirm faith and remind me that I have nothing to fear. They are welcome and when they show up, my heart is filled with joy. But wouldn't it be nice to be so sure, I didn't need them? The signs themselves would be the fruits of authentic Truth about relationships, wealth, wellness, giving and sharing love, knowledge, material objects, purposeful work that feeds you joy, and family togetherness. If I died today, it would be okay. I don't want to die. I don't believe it's going to happen today. But if it does, that's okay. Knowing who I am and living from that space is all that matters because that's what Truth is.

Some lives are short, some are long, some are rough and some are smooth, but each and every life makes up the Divine tapestry of the cosmos. Mitch, you died young. It was a short life and not always enjoyable. You made the choice to leave out of fear or possibly out of love, thinking that we'd be better off without you. To an extent, we are. I think we've become better people because you're not here. I wouldn't have asked for it that way, but it happened. We had to lose you to gain strength and wisdom as individuals and as a family. It's still not always pretty, but we have to move with the change, be that change and let the ever-constant state of change flow through us. We can see it differently and choose to grow, or slump on the couch. We have free will and the choice is always ours. We just need to decide which way we want to go.

I'm walking this way. I'm talking this way. I'm being this way. I choose new beginnings. The stars align when I align with them as the source of the universe. With Anita's story in mind, I wrote a proposal for this book and sent it out to publishing agents in New York and California. Within three days, I got one. A couple of weeks later, Amanda and I were invited to a new friend's house in Beverly Hills for a birthday party where I met our friend's uncle who is chief publisher at a publishing house. The path was opening. I created my website and I blogged and punched out weekly posts on dealing with loss, spiritual growth, and healing. Before long, some of these posts were published online. Then I was invited on podcasts to share my story. The interviews were well received and people started writing to me asking for guidance.

The guidance and support I offered people was greatly appreciated. Such positive results inspired me to start coaching, encouraging people to see their greatest struggles as gifts for inner and outer transformation. Coaching led to speaking engagements at schools and I began running live webinars. The thirst for connection and education led me to research spirituality programs. I applied for an MA Psychology in Education – Mind, Body & Spirituality at Columbia University in NYC. They took only took thirty or forty people from around the world and I was accepted for nothing special besides being me. The path continues to reveal itself step by step. It's not all smooth sailing, but I can handle these gusts of wind.

I wonder what your life would have looked like if you aligned with your loving Truth. I wonder who you would have become. That would have been cool to see. I think you would have given yourself and this world something special. Maybe in the next one. Maybe when you're ready.

I just want people to know that when life falls apart after suicide or personal disaster and they're lost in the dark, there is a way back to the light. I want people to know they have that opportunity. The invitation is there, not only for the lucky ones. It's there for all of us if we can wake up and see things for what they are. It requires that we start again. We have to be willing to see things differently, to start a new conversation and surrender to love. It starts inside when we listen to the pain and struggle. It tells us what we need to know.

Start there and go into it head on. Feel the feeling. With time, with love, with forgiveness, with renewed connection to yourself and universal source energy, you will be grounded in this life. That includes being grounded in death. When you're truly rooted in the circle of life, you can start living your Truth from the heart. There is nothing to fear. Don't be fooled by the tales and torments of the ego and what you've been led to believe. The ego loves to complicate life. You can be angry, sad, frustrated and annoyed, but you don't have to stay there long. Be here, be now, be you, own you, and love you.

In the words of Anita Moorjani – *Love yourself like your life depends on it, because it does.*

Marsh

MITCH TEACHES ME ABOUT THE CHOICE TO BE HAPPY

THE BIGGEST LESSON Mitch taught me was about choice. The choice to be happy. We always have freewill to see things the way we want to. The choice to be happy after suicide loss didn't come overnight. For long periods of time, I chose suffering. It was my choice not to see things differently, but then I committed to growing from the experience. How we deal with obstacles comes down to choice at the most basic level. Now that this has happened, I asked myself, what am I going to do about it?

I recall Wayne Dyer saying, "With everything that has happened to you, you can either feel sorry for yourself or treat what has happened as a gift. Everything is either an opportunity to grow or an obstacle to keep you from growing. You get to choose."

Mitch's passing taught me to focus on all the beauty in life. I chose to see all the reasons in life to celebrate instead of mourn. He taught me that my happiness didn't have to be conditional on anything or anyone. I had the inherent right to be happy but I had to make the decision. For people who have been through suicide loss or any other major life turmoil, there comes a stage when you have to ask yourself, "How badly am I going to let this affect me long term?" If you've made the choice to run away and hide from your suffering, how much longer are you willing to go on like that?

It all comes down to choice. You're entitled to make your own decisions about what you want to feed your heart and mind. However you want to live your life is completely up to you. But if your life continues to be unhappy, if it lacks joy, love, energy, creativity and a hopeful vision of the future, do you want to continue this way? Do you want to keep walking down the same street, falling into the same potholes, wondering where all the lights have gone? Those outcomes are robbing you of a happy life. Wouldn't you like to take a chance and try something different?

Start by keeping it simple. Ask yourself, Do I want to work towards being happy? Yes or no?

Yes.

Well, okay great! But that's going to require change and being willing and open to looking at life, including the past, in a new light. Are you okay with that?

I'm not sure.

Why are you unsure?

Because I don't know if I can change how I think and feel about what happened. It's too painful.

How long have you held onto this pain?

Years.

What if in a year's time you had the opportunity to dissolve your pain and grow from the experience. What would that mean to you?

That would be everything. But I still don't think I can do it.

Are you willing to try?

From here, there is a simple choice. Yes or no. We always have the choice to look at things from a different vantage point. We can be open to life and possibility, or we can be closed. It's that simple. I never said the process was easy. I believe it's simple to understand but hard to do. And yet, it's harder to walk around bearing the cross of suffering and pain produced from the past or the future, neither of which exist.

You don't have to feel guilty about being happy. You have permission to be happy and to be loved and fulfilled. Just understand that whatever you choose to focus on will expand. Creation is an extension of your thoughts. Feed yourself sorrow and suffering and that's precisely what you'll get. Feed yourself hope, self-inquiry, gratitude and love, and see what shows up. Experiment with your life, choose to be unconditionally happy, and see what sunshine brings to your day. For the longest time I resisted happiness because I was so identified with my internal dialogue. Suffering had become so glorified, I used it as a way to manipulate my social environments. In Marianne Williamson's best-selling book based on a Course in Miracles, "A Return to Love," she says:

"People have focused on the crucifixion more than the resurrection. But crucifixion without the resurrection is a meaningless symbol. Crucifixion is the energy pattern of fear, the manifestation of a closed heart. Resurrection is the reversal of that pattern, brought about by a shift in thought from fear to love."

I love this quote and I feel it in my heart. I have lived both sides and I know where I choose to place my focus. In our world today, don't you feel as though it's your responsibility to be happy? Don't you want to come home to your true nature and remove the separation? It's challenging enough dealing with what life throws at us and awakening to the available lessons. Why not choose to be you and only you? Live and breathe your natural inheritance of love. Make the choice to be happy and share it with the world.

LETTER 22:

HEAVEN ON EARTH

September, 2015

Dear Mitch,

Did you ever believe in a heaven on Earth? Did you ever want to understand how nature intended things to be? Did you ever stop to take in the beauty of the ocean where we lived? I wish I could have you back as a child. When I see your face back then, I think about my newfound respect for my body and my surroundings. Your essence was heaven and there was nothing for you to change. All you had to do was be you and to work with life, not against it. As I stand on the shore of the Pacific Ocean in Santa Monica, California, and gaze out to sea, I feel my awareness expand. I feel closer to Oneness. I feel bliss and I feel heaven in my heart. That is why I know life is such a gift. That is why I know heaven is where I'm standing.

This is the best of both worlds. In this life we have the opportunity to create. There are no limits to our creativity when we have a connection to spirit. That connection is the essence of what we long to express through our physical bodies. That much I know. That is what you've taught me. I had to let go of you and I had to let go of fear to remember that. It sounds so simple to "let go" and it is, once you give yourself permission. Remaining distorted by fear makes it extremely challenging to let go. In the distortion and intrusion of fear, there is no room for the awareness of love. For you, Mitch, there was so much interruption, there was no chance to express your true self as the loving force you were meant to be. Did you curse and condemn yourself for failing to meet your own standards?

When we were kids, we led privileged lives. When the disappointments came, was that too much for your fragility? Did you feel exposed? Did that send you into a meta-cognitive tailspin void of meaningful, positive thoughts? Did you engage in your own destruction? Was the future you saw as a kid denied? I've been over this with you before when I think of the power in letting go and surrendering to the flow of life. We'll never know exactly what you couldn't let go of and in this moment it doesn't matter. I just wish you had the opportunity to know the boundless possibilities for your life to experience the best of both worlds when you were alive.

To feel my awareness expand through the act of self-love sends a tingling sensation throughout my body. There is lightness and spaciousness. There is room to receive what self-love reflects back at me. The funny thing is, spaciousness doesn't feel empty. It feels full of energy that can do or be anything. I feel the breath of life fill me up. There is a sense of freedom and peace in this conscious state of awareness. Nothing else matters other than the moment. Thoughts that come to mind have no association. They feel new. I dig my feet deeper into the sand and feel my energy move up to the crown of my head. I release that energy out of the top of my head and for a few seconds I don't feel the need to breathe. When I take my next breath, I fill up my lungs with love and breathe out the words "fear be gone."

It's hard to fathom the gratitude I have in my heart for you, Mitch. I didn't know what was going to happen after you left. I didn't know what my life was going to look like. I didn't know if I'd survive in one piece. I didn't know if my life would resemble someone else's. I was so scared. And now all I have for you is a juicy grin. You gave up your life to teach me about mine. I see that as an act of love and I know you'd be happy for me. Thanks for the gift. I hope you come to realize what death has taught you, whatever that may be. Use those lessons for the next time around. Maybe you'll put them to better use! Sorry, but not sorry. I'm still allowed to give you a jab when I feel you need it!

Be you,

Marsh

REFLECTION:

MITCH TEACHES ME TO BE GRATEFUL

THERE HAVE BEEN times in my life when I lost all sense of gratitude. Like Mitch, in times of confusion, anger and frustration, I was blind, resistant to seeing the good in things. I remained focused on what I thought my life should be, which kept me trapped in the past or too far into the future. I didn't allow myself to enjoy the present moment, which is all we really have.

Without gratitude, our immune systems weaken, we sleep less, and our health suffers. We're less alert, alive, joyful, optimistic, and happy. We feel lonely and isolated, less forgiving and outgoing, less generous and helpful. We sink into overwhelming anxiety about life. Our hearts are closed. We don't feel supported and there is no goodness, gifts, or benefits in our lives. We forget that giving is living and we are on a downward spiral of struggle and resistance to life.

Gratitude is a simple practice, but we don't it take as seriously as we should because of our ingrained psychological tendencies. We can start by being thankful for the small things, from a good night's sleep to the clothes on our backs, having money in the bank to being able to fill up the car with gas. But gratitude is not only about receiving. It is also about giving. Mother Teresa said she was grateful to help the sick and homeless on the streets of Calcutta because they helped her grow. Whether you hold the door open for an elderly lady in an elevator or come to know a valuable lesson through a painful loss, gratitude has transformative effects on our lives.

Gratitude magnifies positive emotions and allows us to celebrate the present moment, which was a struggle for me during my grief. These days, I choose to participate in life and appreciate the value of something on a consistent basis. In essence, I have trained my mind not to take things for granted. Gratitude counteracts the toxic, negative emotions of resentment, envy, and regret. It's almost impossible to feel gratitude and resentment at the same time. They are incompatible feelings, and love always wins.

Some days, I wish I had shown more gratitude in my twenties in the face of trauma and suffering. I have no doubt that a shift in mindset and a practice of gratitude would have made me more stress-resistant. But on the flip side, now that I have learned the lesson, I am stronger and I feel more propelled to interpret negative life events differently. I am grateful that I have a higher sense of self-worth.

Good and bad things will happen to everyone. It doesn't matter who you are. The key is to count your blessings each and every day because you don't know when your time is up. Even if you happen to live to ninety, wouldn't you rather be open and enjoy enjoying each day, rather than seeing your life as a bad hand you've been dealt?

I suggest you keep a gratitude journal and every day, write down five things you're truly grateful for. Sit with those five things and feel them in your heart. If you don't want to write, then stop for a few minutes in the morning and think of five things to be grateful for. Maybe you have kids and you'd like to keep a gratitude jar. Each day, place loose coins and small bills into the jar. When it's full, use the cash to give something. Start with your kids and make it fun. Remember, your kids are the future caretakers of this planet.

After you lose someone to suicide or some other life trauma, it may feel like there's absolutely nothing to be grateful for. That is your pain talking. I understand there's a time to mourn losses, which is different for everyone. But you are digging yourself an early grave if you stay in that place for years on end without seeking the silver lining or the rainbow in the cloud. Even though you're living in the physical sense, you'll be dying on the inside. It doesn't have to be that way. At the end of the day it all comes down to how you want to see things and how willing you are to heal.

I try to ground myself in the circle of life. People will die young, old, through disease, tragedy, or accident. It happens and it's real tough at times. But you have to keep moving because life isn't going to wait for you. Grief is waking you up to move with life, to grow and change with it. Be open to the lessons. Don't separate yourself. Make room for gratitude no matter what your circumstances and keep moving. Keep living. On the other side of your struggle is a stronger connection to love and gratitude for what you have survived.

A NEW SUNDAY LUNCH

February, 2016

Dear Mitch,

Our family is the biggest it's ever been. Matt has two young boys and Morg has his first baby boy. More boys! Will it ever end? It doesn't look that way. I'm the only hope for a girl, I'd say. Give me a few years. It's amazing to see the joy and delight Mum and Dad experience being grand-parents. I don't think I've ever seen Dad play with toy trucks on the floor. It's softened him and in many respects, made him more present. It's quite a sight. To see Mum indulge in as many cuddles as she can handle warms my heart. The dark cloud that hovered over this roof while you were here is gone. We've grown as a family and the new additions breathe fresh life into the energy field, but are some things still the same?

I'm home from Los Angeles for a few months and have taken delight in spending precious time with everyone. This year, many of the friends you grew up with are turning forty. A close friend of ours said, "Why don't we have a fortieth birthday party for Mitch?" I was caught off guard by his question. I hadn't really allowed it to sink in properly when I said, "Yeah, yeah. What a great idea. We should do that."

That night around the dinner table, I thought about the party. I didn't say anything to anyone. Instead I casually engaged in conversation about Mum's cooking and the weather. I was a million miles away in my mind, reflecting on how each family member had dealt with your passing. If a friend hadn't proposed the birthday idea, I wonder if we would have acknowledged it in the first place. I don't recall ever having a birthday celebration in February for you since you died. Would it be weird to celebrate a hypothetical fortieth? Did family members want to be reminded of you among a group of friends that didn't have much to do with you the last six to eight years of your life?

No blemish or judgment on them. You distanced yourself from the crowd. A party may be lovely for those that didn't have to live with you through those years of darkness. In a party environment, they might want to remember and celebrate the good times. Rightly so! Those are the moments we all cherished with you, Mitch. But is the sting still here for family members? Would it be like going into a time warp back to our most horrific memory? I asked myself, "How do I feel about the idea?"

The thing is, Mitch, I've reached a point where your passing is neither sad nor happy. I've moved through the emotional charge. That is not to say I am void of feeling, but I see the upside and the downside to losing you. I've reached a true love and appreciation for you in my life. It is what it is. I see the hidden order.

So, let me rephrase. From my perspective, I'd be happy to have a fortieth celebration for you because it's an opportunity for the family, an invitation to create a new Sunday lunch, so to speak. It's already very different with little munchkins sitting at the table, but I'm talking about watering and nurturing a new conversation where it's okay to say your name loud and say it clear. It can be a memory we loved, an experience we'd like to forget, or we can talk about the impact it had on each of us. I want that type of intimacy to evolve. I see new dimensions in that openness and unity. I see love being shared and the suicide bubble burst once and for all in a free exchange of catharsis. That's my dream. Not to ruffle feathers or to cause turmoil or discomfort. I dream about healing and plugging back power that has been missing from our family's energy circuit.

I come from a place of love and hope these days. But with this dream comes the reality that it's not my job to heal the wounds of others in the family. I can be an example, but I can't do the healing on anyone else's behalf. Who knows? Maybe everyone else has healed and moved on. Maybe I needed the most help and I've gotten transformative meaning from your death. Maybe that's my journey and that's all there is to it. No, I dream of more.

The proposal for the party goes out on email to family and friends. That probably wasn't the smartest idea in hindsight. I was just so determined with my own hopeful agenda that I bypassed a family discussion about it first. The response from close friends was instantly positive. I knew that would be the case. But none of that matters if the family doesn't feel comfortable. That was what Mum told me initially. A few nights later, when she and I got into it, I made a conscious effort to listen to everything she had to say without trying to push my perspective on her. I didn't want her to get defensive if she felt uncomfortable with the situation.

"We had to live with him, Marsh," she said. "The unfortunate reality is that he spent the better part of the last ten years of his life in misery. Going into a room full of people and celebrating a milestone year of the dead is not what I want to do."

"I hear what you're saying, Mum. I'd actually prefer to not call it a fortieth birthday. How about we think of it as a coming together with friends to commemorate Mitch's life?"

"What friends?" she said. "He shut himself off from everybody. I feel uncomfortable. Mitch was a beautiful child, too sensitive for this world, but the upheaval he caused this family was disastrous. I don't want to remember that. I've moved on. I don't want to celebrate that."

This conversation was winding Mum up.

"I think you're missing the point," I said. "I don't think anyone in that room wants to remember the dark days. I thought this would be a good opportunity for the family to talk about it. I don't think it's ever been properly dealt with. We've never talked about it."

"What do you mean? We've talked about him."

"You and I have. I'm talking collectively. I can count on three fingers the times its been openly discussed and never in any deep context."

"You've been off traveling the world haven't you? You're so secretive. Ask your brothers. They say trying to get information out of you is impossible."

"I may not want to divulge what I see as the unimportant details of my life and who I'm dating, but serious, real stuff? Of course I want to discuss that."

We pause and breathe.

"There is no blame or judgment, Mum. That's not what I'm doing. I'm just stating the facts. I thought this would be a healing opportunity for us. Shit, I don't want to be in a room of misery, remembering his depressive state. Are you kidding? This is about family and close friends who knew and loved Mitch, sharing love and breaking bread. I'm seeing this as a good thing, Mum. For everyone. But the last thing I want is for anyone in the family to feel uncomfortable. If that's going to be the case, then I don't think we should go ahead."

Dad had been listening intently from his chair. He was calm and patient, two traits I wouldn't normally associate with him. He could see my motivation. I spoke genuinely and honestly, instead of charging into an argument about we should do this, that, and the other because I said so and it's the right thing to do.

Dad reflected the same authenticity back at me when he said, "We'll have lunch on Sunday and talk about it with everyone and get their feedback. We'll make a decision from there. Okay?"

"Okay."

Sunday came along and we had lunch at Matt's house. The kids were running around, the food was being prepared in the kitchen, light rain was falling outside and the barbeque was heating up on the balcony. Dad took a seat on the living room couch and broached the subject with a clear, calm tone. "Now, about Mitch's thing. Your mother and I have spoken, along with Marsh about what we'd like to do."

"I think it's strange having a fortieth birthday for him," Matt said.

"That's what I thought originally," Dad said. "But I see Marshall's point of view."

"He sees it as more of a celebration with friends to remember," Mum interjected.

"He was a pain in the arse," said Matt. "I don't see why we need to celebrate his birthday if he's not here. So after that, we'll have a fiftieth?"

"Look, I don't think we should do it if people are uncomfortable. Mum?" Morgan asked.

"I'm not as uncomfortable as I was a few days ago. I've come around. I see Marshall's perspective," she said.

"I think it's a nice way to keep his spirit alive," said Morgan. "I don't see it as anything other than that."

"That's all it is," I added.

I could see Matt's point of view. There was no reason to label it a birthday party. In a way, that was irrelevant. This is a time to talk and celebrate you, Mitch, something we hadn't done in a very long time. This is our opportunity as a family to look under that rug and sweep it out. Everyone has a choice to live their lives and see things how they want to see them, but the opportunity for a personal breakthrough could be there for certain family members. Much like this book. They may or may not read it, but if they do, the potential for a shift in thinking is available. The way I see it, this book is just as much for them as it is for me.

"I'd like to do it if everyone else is happy," said Morgan. "Being around old friends makes me feel good. Like he's here."

"Okay," said Dad. "Your mother and I will take another night to think about it."

I sense that there is still a charge in Mum. I have no doubt she's a better person because of losing you, Mitch, but she still doesn't want to be reminded of how you left us. She had to bare the brunt of your depression and erratic behavior. She wore that and had to live with that. We all did to an extent, but Mum is the family's sounding board. At times she has taken on everyone's issues. Over time I can only imagine how depleted that can make a person feel. She's tired and I don't blame her. She deserves to jump on a plane and go to Europe for a month by herself away from all of us. Let her breathe. I can't speak for a mother's loss. I can only comment as your brother and a man who has done the same amount of work as a go-getter puts into building his career, but I did it on myself. I can only speak as a man who has wanted to understand and awaken to the Truth and the laws that govern our universe.

The Truth I see in my heart is that Mum and every other family member has missed the beauty of losing you. Mum's opposition to a party comes from the past that hasn't fully healed. In my eyes, the upheaval and distress you caused with your sad state was one hundred per cent the best thing that could have happened. I believe if we all want to look closer and deeper we can arrive at a place of balance and peace within ourselves. Now we have balance because you're no longer here. Nothing else matters.

There is no need to carry anything. We can let go and detach from you. We can die into this moment with you and be free to love and appreciate what brought us to Now.

Now, we are keeping your spirit alive because you are still a member of our family. I feel it in my body and there is only a lightness of being. The only reason we think grief, suicide and death is bad or negative is because have been taught to believe that. People die. Some people like you, Mitch, didn't want to be here and that's okay. If you decided you wanted to stay and turn things around, that would have been okay, too. But you didn't. You didn't. You left in a moment that is now no longer available to us. Can you show me yesterday?

Growth. I can smell growth out of suffering. The sharp pains of spiritual awakening are tolerable now. They heal the quickest when light shines down on them. The dull ache of a lifetime of holding onto pain is debilitating. There's no escaping it. You choose to know and love the Truth or you don't. You choose to love and appreciate how the struggles have ultimately served you, or you stay asleep in a closed mind. That's what I see. I see my own short time on this Earth as too fucking precious to miss the opportunity to flow with change. To embrace uncertainty. To take what you have given me and implement that into my life so I can be a better person than I was yesterday.

I see now that I can continue to evolve and expand with the world around me. I can swim in that downstream direction. There is no fight or resistance or regret or anticipation. There is only being and the lightness of spirit. A divine recipe to know myself. You gave that to me and I love you for that. I fucking love you for that. That's more than a gift. It's my life. You gave me rebirth in my life. Now I'm laughing because it's true, it's beautiful, and it's what I am bringing into the room at your party because that shit is happening. Amen.

Mum and Dad have come around and warmed to the idea. Dad was very brief. He simply said to me, "We'll go ahead. Email everyone and confirm numbers." It was like a business transaction. I'm happy with their decision. I knew it's a big deal for them but I also feel a hint of excitement in them, although they might not consciously realize it. The vision in my mind's eye is a room full of boisterous laughter, hugs, deep and meaningful conversation, oneness with each other, and heartfelt presence within ourselves. I look forward to what may come on that day.

The next four days rained in Sydney like you wouldn't believe. I used that time to sit at my desk and write. Out the window, Mum's lush green garden was being watered with fat drops falling from the gray sky. In the afternoon of the fourth day, the sun came out. I saw Mum walk outside to inspect her drenched plants and sweep some of the leaves and debris left by the wind. I watched her sweep for a few minutes before I noticed your face. In the reflection of a plastic cylinder that had a pot plant and a white ceramic dove on top of it, I saw the image of your face between overhanging branches and leaves of neighboring plants. You had my attention. It was not a happy face. You weren't smiling. You looked more peeved than anything else, with pursed lips. Your image stared straight at me. I waited for it to go, assuming I was dreaming. I closed the shutters for thirty seconds and reopened them. Nope, you were still there, right in front of Mum and staring at me.

"Mum," I called out.

"Yes?"

"Can you come here please?"

"Hold on," she said. Then she walked into my room.

I stood up. "Sit down and look right there," I told her. "Look at the reflection in the cylinder. See something?"

"No. What should I be seeing?"

"You don't see him?"

"Who?"

"Mitch's face. He's right there. You don't see it?"

"No, I don't."

"Right through there. Here. Are you looking right here?"

"Yes, I am. I'm looking. I can't see a face."

Mum stood up and I sat back down. Nothing had changed for me. I could still see you. Not for a second did I feel delusional in my judgment, nor did I feel Mum was judging me. She placed her hands on my shoulders and said, "I think it's time you put him to rest. I don't think he can sleep while you're still holding onto him."

"But I'm not, I'm…"

"Finish this book and put him to rest. Let him sleep."

She was right. I need to let you sleep. No wonder the face I saw looked so annoyed. Even in death, I don't think you're pretending to have all the answers. I think you're still learning and evolving like the rest of us.

Now that the day of your celebration has arrived, Sydney has turned on one of her magic days. She is perfect with her rays of sunshine that sparkle like diamonds on the ocean out to the horizon. She has delivered this wonderful gift of togetherness as family and childhood friends gather to remember the good times we shared with you. We're perched above Manly Beach on a gorgeous Sunday morning, breaking bread with loved ones we've known for thirty plus years. That type of friendship is rare, and I am forever grateful. Experiences we've shared with these people run the entire gamut of life's offerings.

It is so special to have loved and supported each other through loss, financial hardship, family breakdowns, and personal suffering. We also share the laughter, adventure and mischief. You were and always will be a part of that world, Mitch. Here we are in a beautiful room with a view of the Pacific Ocean on Sydney's most spectacular of summer days, keeping you in our hearts with a lightness of being and speaking your name with cherished fondness.

Brunch is served in a large open-air balcony where we felt your being carried on the breeze. TV screens are assembled and I play a photo album on repeat full of classic pictures of you, the angel we had the privilege of knowing. There are photos of you and Dad on the beach in Hawaii, you and Mum at Disneyland, you and Matt as toddlers and then at Disneyworld having breakfast with Chip n' Dale. There are proud rugby photos, portraits I'd forgotten about, shots in Portugal I've never seen before, and others with snowboards with your early nineties undercut. I put together forty photos for what would have been forty years on the physical plane. There isn't a sour face in the house. How can there be? There is nothing but love in this room. The past isn't being denied. It is being embraced. All of our apprehensions fade away. Everyone has big, bright smiles and we all feel alive and happy. And so do you.

Being in the room reminds me of a line in *A Course in Miracles:*
Nothing real can be threatened.
Nothing unreal exists.
Herein lies the peace of God.

The aliveness in the room is the energy of love. The love in this room can't be threatened. You are in this room too, a part of the aliveness and love. The essence of you cannot be threatened. It cannot die or be diminished. The grief our family has suffered is illusory, because fear cannot exist. The all-encompassing love I feel and witness nails it home deeper within me than ever before. Relationships never die. The world beyond what I can see is becoming more real to me in this room. I feel the Truth penetrate me in a way I haven't felt before.

It feels like unconditional love is life's golden ticket. I can be as expansive, creative and boundless as I want. In this room I feel full of myself. Not as an ego, but full of the realness, the essence of my being. It fills up my physical container and all I feel is love. How can there be room for anything else?

It's a special day. I'm glad we've come together to celebrate you. You deserve it. What a beautiful lesson to learn on a crystal clear summer's day that our pretty Sydney has delivered just for us.

It's almost time to put you to bed. You got time for one more?

Marsh

REFLECTION:

MITCH TEACHES ME ACCEPTANCE

I'VE BEEN CHALLENGED with various levels of acceptance since Mitch's death. I've had to accept that everyone grieves differently and to varying degrees. I've had to accept a new reality that is permanently devoid of Mitch. Although I know nothing is permanent, the impermanence of life is shocking and at the same time comforting. It's shocking that death can show up at any time, to any of us. It's comforting because it's a natural part of life. Most of all, I now know that the vast majority of my makeup is energy, which can't be broken, so I can never really die.

According to the world's foremost experts on grief, the late Elizabeth Kubler-Ross and author David Kessler, the fifth stage of grief is acceptance. I've been forced to readjust to a life that doesn't include my loved one. It took me quite a while to accept Mitch's death, but even longer to accept the fact that I allowed myself to sink into fear. I'm offering my story now to inspire others who have shared similar life struggles, as I encourage them to take the high road to healing. If I were willing to see things differently earlier on, if I'd been brave enough to address my fears surrounding Mitch's death, I could have moved on with life far sooner.

Acceptance makes me strong, more grounded and rooted in life and my place in it. Acceptance has taught me to love life, to praise it. Death has shown me what is most important in life. To me, it's not happiness, success, or maturity. The more I reflect, the more I accept that the source of my love for life is the fact that it ends. It doesn't frighten me any more.

It liberates me because I know I have to honor the life I've been given. I am motivated to give praise to my life, feed it love, and cherish my joy.

When we view death as a source of love for life, its hard not to enjoy the gift. We've been blessed with sensorial pleasures: the ability to see, smell, listen, touch, and taste. We have the capacity to be self-aware. When we consciously connect with our inner witness, we are reminded of what's around the corner, so we can make the most of today. When we keep that in mind, we can see how insignificant the trivial matters of modern life really are.

I often think back to the day when I saw Mitch's reflection in a plastic cylinder in the garden. Mum told me to finish this book, put Mitch to rest, and let him sleep. She reminded me that life goes on even though he doesn't. I had to accept the fact that nothing I hold dear lasts forever, a reminder to be present, to feel more, to deepen my awareness, and to be more human. Mitch taught me to love the end as much as the beginning and the middle. He taught me that life requires death in order for it to continue, that death feeds everything that lives. Through the pain of suicide, grief has taught me to be grateful for the good and the bad and see how each has benefited me along my path.

It's funny, this thing called life. It makes us laugh, cry, scream, sing, celebrate, and mourn. We have to accept that we're not immune to the bad, that we have the choice to make meaning of our lives. Whichever direction we take, we need to accept our decisions and keep moving because life doesn't wait for anyone. Death has taught me to love today, so I love the shit out of it, I have some fun, and I make the most out of what I have.

LETTER 24:

YOU ARE THE GREATEST GIFT

March, 2016

Dear Mitch,

When I think back on my life, I consider myself very lucky. I've had many great teachers and I hope I encounter many more. Each of these teachers has given me valuable lessons to learn and live by. They have shown up at precisely the right time. Some have come when the sun was shining and some have come when clouds loomed overhead. It's easy to praise the ones that showed up when the sun was out. They will always be priceless to me. Their lessons of humility, focus, and perseverance have served me well. On the other hand, the rainbow in the clouds, as Dr. Maya Angelou said, are also special.

As a family we were blessed with you for twenty-six years. Your death became the rainbow in my cloud. You are my greatest teacher. Did you know that? Well, now you do. All my teachers have been rainbows in sun or clouds. Your rainbow, however, was the biggest and the brightest. The pot of gold at the end of that rainbow has been my healing. Your rainbow is love and love liberates. Love rescues. Love is the Truth. Love has given me the opportunity to see the hidden order, balance, and blessing in your passing. Your rainbow has opened my heart to know myself. You've given me permission to go inside and look, to remove the barriers to my authentic self, to reconnect to the unconditional energy of love. That kind of exploration handed me a paintbrush to paint whatever picture I wanted in my external, physical environment. My world is an expression of that love, for without you I may not have had the opportunity to truly remember.

You taught me that understanding life is simple. But not easy. You taught me to take up the battle and live my life, to make my own choices to create my world in my authentic Truth. That is the right thing to do. That is the only thing to do. I know that now because of you. Can you imagine receiving that type of gift from someone? I mean, hello. What a gift. What a miracle. You are my miracle. Who knew? My brother who walked away from us. My brother who walked away from himself without knowing that his life was worth living. My brother who caused so much perceived suffering and heartache to each of us. Yes, you are my rainbow, my greatest gift of all.

You taught me that death is a progression of life. As spiritual activist, Stephen Jenkinson, says, "It's the end of life that gives life a chance." It doesn't bother me anymore about how you left, although it makes the return to love more challenging. If you had died of a terminal disease, or in a freak accident that was no one's fault, the sting may not have been as great. But now, I see a continuous rebirth and evolution in death, not an end that enables me to die into each moment and let go into uncertainty. It helps me to love each moment for what it is and to know that my time on this Earth is precious.

My only mission now is to give back the love that brought me here. I am here to expand with life and to continuously live my Truth. I want to be the best human I can be, the best version of myself and I want to live what I teach. "Prepare to be a rainbow in someone else's cloud," Dr. Maya Angelou said. That's what it feels like when you don't fear death as the end. That's what it feels like when you can see the blessing in suffering. That's what it feels like when you recognize an opportunity to grow, to move with life, and to flow with change. That's what it feels like when you are connected to yourself and to love. That is the ultimate inspiration, the ultimate calling. That is where you find infinite energy to drive you each and every day in whatever you do and wherever you go. To the office, to church, to temple, to the classroom. Wherever you go, take love with you and give it away. Love liberates. Love rescues. Love is the Truth.

I believe I've never been given anything I couldn't handle. I thought I couldn't handle your suicide. I was wrong. You are not forgotten. You never will be. You live on in my heart and I share what you have taught me. I have no attachment to you, but there is no separation. There are no more tears, only love and gratitude. That's the Truth. May this blessing be a blessing for others. May the light on this page be your resurrection and your redemption. May you see that the gift you left behind is being used for love. You are loved, you always were, and forever will be.

Thank you for teaching me what grief is. Grief is guidance! I refuse to get lost in the perception of separation. It's a trap! Grief isn't just sadness. It's waking me up to who I am and there is no reason on Earth to separate myself from who I am.

I thought your suicide was a complete loss for a long time, but I was separated from love. You merged back with the unconditional energy of love that brought you here. You were free of resistance, you were dancing with the other souls, but I was disconnected and out of alignment with myself while the benefits were staring me in the face. My relationship with you changed and that was sad for me. It was my choice to suffer because I had been taught that relationships don't continue when someone is gone. No one told me how hard it would be to define the gap between the physical and spirit. I had to get out of touch with myself and disconnected from love in order to decide that I didn't want to feel this way anymore.

Your passing opened up a whole new, richer relationship that is more in sync and unified now than ever before. How on Earth could I have possibly had this type of relationship with you if you were alive and in depression? Every relationship you had, including the one with yourself, was backwards. Grief clogged up the toilet. Being connected to love flushed it away. All it took was a choice. You released all your resistance. All I had to do was release mine.

There are lots of messages that instruct us not to celebrate a suicide or any other type of loss. But I see now that you're free. All the baggage is gone. You're back in blissful alignment. Isn't that good enough for reason for celebration? You've got your power back, right? Why is that a bad thing? I need to find a different label for suicide and death, because what's out there can seriously fuck with your mind. I want to call it "The Homecoming Party." Now that all the resistance is gone and you're at peace with who you are, you have stronger, deeper access to me and vice versa. Now we have meaning. Now we have beauty in our relationship. I am not alone without you. You are not alone without me. I am alone when I diminish the connection of who I am, not because you are gone.

To be perfectly honest, I never actually missed you that much. You were a royal pain in the arse most of the time, like Matt said. I missed the connection with myself. I kept thinking that something very bad happened to create this awful explosion of emotions that kept me powerless. But in the end, your death was guidance. You made your way back home with spirit and gave me a roadmap to connect with mine in my physical body. Big brother, do you know how good it feels to be in this body and know love? Exhilaration☺ Laughter☺ Gratitude☺ Awareness☺. These are your gifts. You helped me remember the brilliance within me. All I can say is thank you. And all I can do is live it and share it with the world.

Love liberates. Love rescues. Love is the Truth.

I love you,

Marsh

LIFE IN THE LOVE LANE

THINGS EVENTUALLY DO get better. There is a way out of the pain. I'm standing here to tell you that there is a way out, but you will need to muster your courage to heal yourself. No one can to do it for you. Your courage and willingness to connect to source energy will carry you out of this. You are more than capable of doing it. Even in the worst of pain and the darkest of hours, there are healing discoveries that can take you to a different place. In my heart of hearts, I know there is an opportunity for you to feel good again. I truly hope that my story has provided sparks of inspiration and hope for the future. There is new life that arises out of your love and gratitude for who you've lost and what you've been through. The impact this experience has had on your life, what you have learned and how you have grown, can make you a better person.

I'm thirty-four now and hopefully I have many years in front of me. A lot has happened since Mitch died. I'm happy in my life right now. I'm happy about what I've discovered about myself and my unique contribution to this world. I love that. I wish there was an easier, less scary and confronting path to this awakening, one in which Mitch was back with us living a happy, healthy and prosperous existence. There are days I wonder about that. I don't dwell on it but I'd be lying if I said that I didn't hope for that.

That didn't happen, though, and life gave me what it gave me. This is my story, my journey, and it's still happening without Mitch in it. The deeper part of me is grateful for him. I can hardly express my gratitude because I don't know what I'd be doing with my life if he were still alive. Whatever that alternate universe looks like, I can tell you that it wouldn't be as connected to spirit as it is now. That is the biggest take away. Being connected to my spirit and knowing what feeds it joy, means everything to me and I feel that life will continue to open up to me. I feel like a part of the collective whole. I don't feel separate from anyone or anything. I understand my place in the world. I am an important piece, just like you. I have a purpose and contribution to this world, no matter how long or short my physical life may be.

I like to see myself in other people. I love to learn from them and hear their stories. I love to stop, look and listen so I can be present in my environment, wherever I am. I love to say thank you. Thank you, God, for giving me this life. I am alive but life isn't only about me. We are all in this together. It took the death of Mitch, my elder brother, a beautiful, sensitive guy with so much promise and love to give, for my awakening to occur. I'll never forget him and what he has given me.

I still remember thinking that my heart would never be healed from losing Mitch. I'm not saying that I'm over it. He's my brother and a part of my history. I don't want to get over him. But I have learned to use him as a catalyst to look deeper, to become more intimate with myself and with life. In that way, I have learned to let go. I have also learned that suffering always leads back to love.

We all have to do this hard thing for ourselves. But it's worth it because the more work, self-inquiry and reflection, the more I honor the life I've been gifted, the more Mitch's death becomes a guide to living. He gave me a guide to life. That's what suffering is. And it has led me to what I call "Life in the Love Lane." I'm talking about life with all the bells and whistles, the ups and downs, dissolving the fears, standing up after I've been knocked down, shining a light on the dark, being a light for others, experiencing creation, being equally impressed with birth and death, and being in awe of both. It means there's a time to cry and laugh, to be happy and sad, to enjoy the fruits of success and the lessons of failure, to know that grief is guidance, a natural process of loss that needs to be felt fully, no matter how intense the pain.

Life in the Love Lane means taking risks and stepping into the unknown, trusting that everything will work out for the best. It means knowing that the love of a Higher Power brought me here, as I return the favor and truly honor that gift. It means developing and nurturing relationships. It means being grateful for the family I have and for what I've done. I try not to take life too seriously and have fun wherever I can, no matter what the pressure or circumstances I'm no longer afraid of my number being called because I know that I'm being taken care of, now and eternally.

I believe that a Higher Power is working with me now, begging me to own my essence, my gifts and abilities, so I can enjoy the ride this time around. I am enough as I am. I am whole and I can make this world what I want it to be. I have choices. And I have made the choice to write this book to offer hope and inspiration to others who are suffering through suicide loss or any other major life obstacles. That's Life in the Love Lane – warts and all.

Finally, I know your heart is broken. You may be hurting so badly, you can't see a way out but I promise you that there is one and things will get better. You are always connected to the light and love that you need. In time and with the willingness to get real with yourself and be present, you can heal your life. When you are ready and willing, the God in you will mend your broken wings. When the time comes to fly once more, you'll see life from a new vantage point and be forever grateful for what you have been through.

All my love,

Marshall

Family portrait – Sydney, 1988

(Left to right) Morgan, Matthew, Mitchell and Marshall.

Mitchell William Dunn – 24/2/1976 – 1/10/2002

ACKNOWLEDGEMENTS

FIRST AND FOREMOST, I want to thank my parents, Jill and Kerry, for all their love and support in this lifetime. I couldn't have asked for better parents, in all honesty. I feel truly blessed to have shared so many great memories over the years. We've experienced our fair share of rough times, but they've been equally matched with the good. It has been quite a journey, one which has helped mold this book and who I am today. Thank you so much. I love you guys.

To my brothers, Matthew and Morgan, thanks for being the amazing people that you are. I hope there's something in this book for you to reflect upon and consider on your own journeys. Love you guys.

I want to thank my editor, Andrea Cagan, who did a fantastic job of tightening up the manuscript and making it as focused as possible. It was an absolute pleasure working with you. I also want to thank my incredible partner, Amanda who has been my rock throughout this process. Thank you for your patience, your unwavering love and support and your advice when I needed it.

To my great mate, Daniel Ucchino, thank you so much for your help when I needed it the most and pushing me to dig deep. I'm so grateful for your friendship and generosity.

Thank you to my dear friend, Zena Nzibo, for helping me proof read the manuscript. Your keen eye and notes are so greatly appreciated. I want to give a shout out to my close friends who I've shared intimate conversations with over the years about the journey through suicide loss – thank you to heaven and back.

Lastly, I want to thank God – a universal, loving presence, which to me exists within all sentient beings. Your infinite power has allowed me to be an instrument of creativity. Thanks for helping me write this book, it was a pleasure working with you.

ABOUT THE AUTHOR:

MARSHALL DUNN coaches individuals around the world to manifest their visions for the lives they were born to live. He is dedicated to help raise humanity's consciousness and be a leader for those looking to follow their soul's purpose.

For more information, please visit www.marshalldunn.com.

33747512R00125

Made in the USA
Middletown, DE
17 January 2019